IN YOUR HANDS

Mark Emme

IN YOUR HANDS

*The Everyman's Guide
to Masturbation*

BRUNO GMÜNDER

1st edition

© 2013 Bruno Gmünder Verlag GmbH

Kleiststraße 23-26, D-10787 Berlin

info@brunogmuender.com

Original title: De la masturbation

© Mark Emme

Translation: Nicholas Andrews

Cover photo: © Marc Drofmans

Printed in Germany

ISBN 978-3-86787-524-0

More about our books and authors:

www.brunogmuender.com

Contents

Foreword

Let repressed hypocrites turn away from this book in a huff: one hundred fifty pages devoted to the infamous vice that led a scandalized Yahweh to punish Onan! One hundred fifty pages that could very well fall into the hands of innocent youths! When will such books finally be forbidden—and where are the police when you need them?

But all other readers can be glad: all those who have good relationships with their own bodies, who know that the body is their most reliable and generous friend, all those who don't turn red at their body's demands, but instead grab hold of the opportunity with relish!

The possibilities of getting to know oneself better are not, after all, so numerous that they should be lazily left unattended. We should praise the author's altruism—he would have made a good student of old Socrates. What a shame that Socrates—not only a philosopher but also a sensualist—can't read this book. He would have been proud to see how literally Mark Emme has taken his credo "know thyself."

Did I say altruism? But what does self-gratification have to do with gracious thoughts towards others? Mark Emme has succeeded in solving this paradox: sure, his "field research" clearly gave him a lot of enjoyment; but then, with what patience and stubbornness did he sit down afterwards to write down and explain the techniques he developed for male self-gratification in all their minute details! With what strictness and scientific devotion did he dedicate himself to his pedagogical task!

In this book, Mark Emme isn't content to satisfy the reader's curiosity with a few banal masturbation recipes—which wouldn't be bad in itself, if you think of the general illiteracy that reigns in this field. He sees self-gratification as an entire sexual world with fertile, over-exploited regions and unexplored areas; with mountainous steppes and oases of abundance. A world whose center is the penis, and whose most beautiful creation is the orgasm. A world in which a man, driven by curiosity as much as the joy of lust, will not cease exploring until his bodily powers abandon him. No guide could make finding orientation in this world easier than Mark Emme's. None of our strengths or weaknesses escapes him: he knows how to suppress the premature "flood of sperm," but also how an exhausted penis can reach new power. He knows everything about the sensibilities of our various skin regions and knows how to combine the pleasure of touch with visual pleasure. Not even the mechanisms of our psyche and its effects on our sexuality are foreign to him. He is, among us poor ignorami, a wise man reaching out his hand to help us.

Some readers might ask why this whole book deals exclusively with men and male self-gratification.

Certainly, women as well as men deserve access to the innocent pleasure of self-gratification—but no one could seriously reproach Mark Emme for being merely a man and not a hermaphrodite. Maybe at some point in the future a woman will appear who will render her services toward researching female self-gratification with as much skill as Mark Emme.

Despite such objections, it goes without question that this book will soon be considered a milestone. It's also certain that it will become bedtime reading for countless readers. So let us praise the Great Masturbator!

Guillaume Fabert

Introduction

This work is split into three chapters:

—the first deals exclusively with the erection itself
—the second deals with various masturbation exercises
—and the third finally leads, through various exercises and
control tests of willpower, to ejaculation

The exercises in this book are intended for all men, whether young or old. For most, they will be a revelation. Splitting the book in three parts makes it easier for readers to confront the two biggest problems of male sexuality: erectile difficulties and premature ejaculation.

In order to test the exercises in this book, you should be naked and allow yourself lots of time and quiet. You should free yourself from all compulsions, anxieties, and prejudices.

All the exercises are written in "real time," which is to say in the time it takes to carry them out. For this reason alone they are guaranteed to be "authentic": after all, they have been "experienced." Because most of the exercises include commentary and descriptions of the sensations corresponding to each action, you will notice when the moment is right how authentically I have proceeded.

Of course, it's impractical and not exactly exciting to carry out the exercises I've described while holding the book in your hand. The best thing to do is to read them once all the way through and then to re-enact from memory the grips described. Then if you don't remember one of the methods exactly, you can pick the book up at any time as a guide. But in the end you'll find out that practice makes perfect, and you'll soon be able to master the individual techniques.

While some of the grips or strokes for stimulation and self-gratification might seem outlandish or even boring to you, someone else might find those movements quite thrilling. As much as we are similar to one another, we're each quite different as well! Nevertheless I have no doubts that you'll enjoy putting many of these exercises into practice.

They are all the result of a long apprenticeship and countless experience. But if I had confined myself to that, this book would certainly have never come into being. All the exercises were additionally examined thousands of times for reliable effectiveness, so I could be certain that they were more than just a matter of personal preference and could offer broad-reaching assistance.

If you've been masturbating without your partner's knowledge up until know, now would be a good time to tell him or her. It's the only way you can free yourself from any lingering feelings of guilt. Only when you truly liberate yourself from within can you open up and become aware of a sensuality that has perhaps escaped you in the past. Later on, it will be easy for you to pass on your knowledge.

After you've tried all the exercises, you will find that this book has revealed an entirely new sexuality to you. A sexuality which—in the age of AIDS—has the advantage of being entirely risk-free and safe!

How Can I Overcome Difficulties with My Erection?

Lots of men simply lack imagination. They always masturbate by the same rules without ever trying something new, without ever improvising.

Most of them only behave this way because they're afraid: by the age of forty, and often much earlier, many men become almost pathologically concerned about their erections. If they have one, only one thing counts: to finish as soon as possible—and then they always complain that they can't hold out longer. Because they want to reach a successful "ending" at all costs, they cheat themselves out of the best moments, the true essence. For this reason alone, it's important to be as relaxed as possible for these exercises in direct stimulation.

Before you begin, remind yourself that this is a game. Self-gratification can be very pleasant once you understand that it's not target-oriented, that it's all about enjoying yourself—and it's not mandatory either. Even if you're not happy with the results, it's not such a big deal. It just means you're not in the right state at the moment to really get into it. Or you can't manage to free your mind of social or acquired pressures. Or you just think this is all idiotic and that stroking yourself is not your thing.

If this last statement is true, you've got false pride: what you're actually most afraid of is making a fool of yourself.

Maybe you believe that such behavior is only appropriate for adolescents who are eager for new sensations. Remind yourself how inexperienced you are, or perhaps try harder to find a way back to your childhood spirit. Then everything could be much simpler. You should also remind yourself that these exercises are not the product of a sick mind. That in fact they've already withstood tests, and that—even if you're skeptical—they actually work! But in order to truly overcome your mistrust, it's absolutely essential that you be alone while you're "learning."

Bit by bit you will see what a pleasure it can be to stimulate yourself thoroughly, rather than simply making use of an erection that—due to a video or porn picture – results from visual arousal. It is then that a whole world of new, unexpected experiences will reveal itself to you.

Too many men still assume that an erection is a purely automatic phenomenon. So they handle a penis that doesn't want to become erect in a totally uptight way, with no sensitivity. Of course it can happen that the mere presence of a particular person can lead to an erection, even if their affections are rather awkward. But well-meant efforts are often rewarded with no success at all. A handsome face or an exciting body can't always make up for complete ignorance of the various stimulation points of the male sex. Sometimes miracles can happen, when someone who might look less enticing knows their way around the body better …

Nothing can replace technique: the pleasure only increases the more you know what you're doing.

A last piece of advice before you start with the first exercises: pay close attention to the smallest sensations your hand and your cock transmit to you. It's possible that a certain stimulation is perfect for your right hand, while the left might obtain a less satisfactory result. On the other hand, it's also possible that it's more convenient to use the left hand for an action that doesn't seem intended for it, if the right has already been performing the action for a long time. This way you can extend arousal a bit by first abating it. It's also possible that you won't enjoy an exercise with the hand I've written. Don't hesitate to try it with your other hand. Maybe this will help you reach the result I'm describing. Lefties will, of course, have to make the necessary adjustments for themselves—which is to say they will use their left hand when I say the right, and vice versa.

My exercises frequently mention foreskin. It's self-evident that those actions can only be included if you're uncut.

Last but not least, it's possible that there are details in my descriptions that don't 100% apply to you. With a little imagination and very minor adjustments to what I've described, you might be able to awaken a sensual harmony that has previously slumbered within you.

1st Exercise

Sit on the edge of your chair, fully upright, your thighs spread wide. Your balls and cock should hang down totally loose. Take a look at them. If you're uncut, it's unimportant whether the foreskin is pulled back or not, since arousal is built up in the shaft to begin with. Even if your foreskin is pulled back at the beginning, it will automatically cover up your dick head later. Place your hands left and right of the base of your cock—fingers extended on top of one another as close as possible to your balls—and point your cock up vertically so that your closed fingers form a kind of support for it.

Then do as follows:

As you move your left hand upwards, your still fully flaccid penis will automatically be pressed against the hollow space formed by the fingers of your right hand. Then you return your left hand to its starting point. Now you repeat this action with right and left hands.

These gestures need to be performed slowly at first, around two per second, but they should be quite firm. Your fingers should move quite quickly up and down the side of your penis very evenly. Don't pause between the gestures. Only your fingertips should touch one another. Make sure that your index fingers are supporting your penis; since it's still flaccid, it will otherwise fall between your thighs.

Keep doing these grips for about a minute (around 120 times back and forth). While you're doing them, observe yourself. Your legs should remain spread wide.

During this preparation you should feel a light hardening, particularly if you push your stomach forward. Now it's time to go faster—not gradually, but right away. You will feel a tingling in your inner thigh. Don't just toss around your cock with your fingertips now, use the first two joints of your fingers. Each time you should hear a clear slapping sound. Pull your stomach in. Through this acceleration and the decisive, firm rubbing, your member will grow larger. Spread your thighs and hold your breath; your balls will start to move upwards. And now go faster and faster—not much longer now to erection!

2nd Exercise

Now assume a somewhat more relaxed sitting position in a comfortable chair by placing your buttocks in the middle of the seat, your arms relaxed with your hands touching your thighs. Let your head fall back relaxed. Keep your eyes closed. It's absolutely necessary that you be completely relaxed for all of these exercises. These preparations for sexual activity can only be truly arousing in a state of full physical and mental relaxation. If you're tired or stressed, you should leave these exercises until later. If your body and mind aren't connected harmoniously, you can't perceive your own sensations with the necessary sensitivity. Or worse: out of nervousness, you maneuver yourself into a cramp that hinders you from getting rid of your tensions through arousal.

Always breathe slowly and deeply; only when your heartbeat grows even and you feel yourself being calm can you begin to stimulate yourself. If you haven't already, you should take your pants off now.

While your hands are touching your half-spread thighs, lay your thumbs on top of one another, about a centimeter below the glans, on the top side of your cock. Lay your index fingers on the underside of your penis at the same height as your thumbs.

Now start massaging the glans by pushing your thumbs upward and your index fingers downward, as if you were winding up a clock. Inevitably, the foreskin will move over the edge of the glans. Then carry out the countermotion in the opposite direction, always very regularly and with little pressure. The four fingers involved here shouldn't change their position during the movements. Your other fingers should simply rest in your palms.

After about 30 or 60 of these back-and-forth motions, you will feel your penis markedly swelling. Your thumbs will be tense, thus pulling less foreskin over the glans.

Continue this motion by exerting stronger pressure with your fingers. This will increase stimulation. Now gradually pull your index fingers further down with each stroke. The motion should become jerkier over time, and clearly directed downwards since your index fingers will be doing most of the work while your thumbs are just making the countermotion. By the way, don't direct your cock downwards while you're doing this, do the opposite: hold it as if you were trying to press it into your own stomach. From then on you'll see how it's clearly grown larger. Now close your thighs, press them together without hurting your balls (which will be half trapped), and let your finger movements become harder, firmer, and more jerky.

At this point you should observe yourself. This will increase your arousal even more. Press your knees tightly together, tense your stomach and ass muscles; your glans will be quite dark already, your penis at its full size. Maintaining the same speed, press your thumbs down more firmly as they rub against the edge of your glans. At the same time, stretch out your legs (still pressed together) and cross your feet. And you'll see: what an erection!

3rd Exercise

In order for a stimulation to be effective, it obviously must be carried out for a certain amount of time. You should avoid changing from one method of stimulation to another too quickly. Make sure you've gotten a chance to truly savor the previous arousal to the fullest. Difficulties are often best solved with a detour! Though it may be necessary to stimulate your penis directly in order to reach erection, the direct way is far from the most effective.

Here's another exercise that leads quickly to an erection, with the advantage that the hand quickly reaches the position it would typically take in "classic" masturbation. This exercise can be performed sitting as well as standing, and is particularly well-suited for "apathetic" cocks and small balls. If you would rather remain seated, you've got to sit right at the edge of your chair in order to perfectly follow the exercise.

Don't forget to relax entirely from the head down!

Sit upright and spread your legs as far apart as possible. During two-thirds of this exercise you should keep your eyes closed in order to keep your arousal in check.

If you're uncut, pull your foreskin back. Lay the palm of your right hand on your inner thigh. Then place your right thumb and index finger just in front of the glans. The other fingers of this hand should be stretched out. Position your left thumb and index finger to the left and right of the base of your cock. Your left thumb should be on the right side of your cock.

With those two fingers, exert steady pressure on your penis while pulling downwards. Instead of sticking upright, your member should stay parallel to your thighs.

As soon as you've taken up this position, start making very fast shaking motions with your right hand—up and down via the wrist, keeping your forearm still. The quicker your two barely-pressed-together fingers move against your glans, the more you will feel the stimulation. Your cock will grow longer and stiffen very quickly. At the same time, you should increase the pressure of your fingers at the base of your cock, continuing to pull them downwards. In order to keep up this rhythm without interruption and to keep your penis from slipping between your middle, ring, and pinky fingers, press these fingers to your palm. Now erection has nearly been reached.

4th Exercise

It is evidently easier for many men to get a hard-on while standing. Position yourself, standing upright firmly on both legs, naked, with your feet about a foot apart. Look at your cock. You need to get used to keeping a cool head at this sight, no matter how turned on you are. That's the only way your muscles can remain relaxed. At first it's certainly not easy, but after awhile you'll be able to control yourself.

Now peel the foreskin back from the glans and test with your hand to see if your ass is truly relaxed.

Place three fingers of your right hand on your penis: your middle finger on the underside of the glans, your stretched-out index finger just in front of the tip of your cock, and your thumb on the top side of your member—in the middle, without really setting it down. Your left hand should lie loosely on your left ass cheek in order to make sure it stays quite relaxed.

Shake your penis slowly up and down—not too firmly—with the two free fingers of your right hand. This gentle movement will push the top side of your cock against your thumb. After about 50 "beats" you will feel your penis growing hard. At the same time, you'll notice your ass and thighs tensing. Relax yourself and don't think about blowing your load! What you're aiming for here is comfortable stimulation. If you notice your member growing harder, you can shake it harder without laying your thumb on it. From this point on, the glans will knock against the tip of your index finger. After a few seconds, this knocking will cause a light pain. This is a good sign: the pain will give way, and if you continue to do this with relaxed buttocks, your cock will soon be erect.

5th Exercise

Some of these exercises are more of a turn-on than others. A few of them are ideal for getting an erection as quickly as possible. Some of them are arousing, but require more stamina. And with others you might have the impression that they're not particularly recommendable—or that they're even a total turn-off.

But in order to know what's good for you, you've got to try everything out first—and more than once, since a technique might work poorly one day and be just the right thing the next.

Don't underestimate the importance of being exact with the hand grips described here. If you understood something wrong, the result might be disappointing. Every detail is important: a finger placed too far up or pressed too firmly at a particular moment can produce the opposite of the intended effect. Never forget that even the smallest changes can bring about the desired result.

The exercise I'm about to suggest can be very arousing while standing, but a bit of a disappointment if you're lying down. But careful: it might sound simple, but this exercise requires lots of sensitivity and a flexible wrist.

With the fingertips of your right hand, grasp your fully flaccid penis from above, directly beneath the glans so that your thumb comes to lie on the top side of your cock (this also holds true if your partner is doing the stimulating). Now bring your cock to a horizontal angle and lay your left thumb and index finger left and right next to the base of the cock.

Your right wrist should be quite loose and relaxed, almost forming a right angle with your forearm.

Now make a quick, vibrating motion with your right hand. Your fingertips should touch your cock very gently. Arousal should come not from the pressure of your fingers, but from the short jerking motions. Your fingers are only there to keep your penis horizontal and to pass on the vibrations coming right from your wrist. If you're able to continue these increasingly fast, light vibrations regularly, you will feel a kind of tingling in the sensitive area around your cock head.

While you're doing this, hold the two fingers at the base of your cock firmly enough that they form a ring around the base, making the skin tight.

Every two or three seconds, grasp tighter with your fingers, imperceptibly slipping backwards. Your cock will grow larger. Now you need to double the speed without changing the amount of pressure. Your member will grow even larger and the vibrations should become jerky. When the penis grows hard, your fingers will almost automatically have less contact with it. Now they've almost become an obstacle rather than holding on to it. You've nearly reached erection …

6th Exercise

Take your penis in your left hand with your four fingers on the underside of the shaft and only the fingertips touching. Your thumb should rest, without pressing down, on the top side of your cock in the middle.

Now press very gently with all five fingers: your thumb will lie on your cock and slide down the shaft, while on the underside only the index finger—lying just beneath your cock head at the frenulum—will exert a counter-pressure upwards.

Repeat this light pressure about twice per second, bringing your cock nearly to a right angle.

After a few seconds, you'll feel arousal again. Your penis will begin to swell. Maintain the rhythm, but press more firmly.

At this point, you won't have much longer to wait before the effect can be felt. Now move your thumb about an inch back, between the base and middle of your cock. The position of your index fingers will change too: now the middle of your index finger should be lying beneath the glans, while the tip of the finger should nestle against the right side of the cock head. Repeat the same stimulation as before without picking up speed, but press more firmly with your thumb. Close your index finger around the glans, causing your cock to be pushed up at an angle, really "bent."

While your penis swells, continue making shorter, harder strokes with your thumb and index finger. Your cock will get harder, so your index finger won't be able to stay in its place. Instead, move it a bit downward, but keep making the same motion, increasing in force. Because the penis is now knocking against the inside of your hand, where the thumb and index finger meet, the stimulation will be greater. As you keep speeding up your hand motion and your penis grows harder, your other fingers will slip a bit to the right side of the shaft, supporting your index finger's movements by giving more pressure. Interrupt any stimulation as soon as your glans becomes dark, but keep your hand in its position. Content yourself simply to think about something else. It will take about half a minute for your erection to subside.

Then start stimulating again: this time it won't take so long for results to show. By making the same movements at a greater speed, you'll reach a perfect erection.

But if you want to increase your pleasure, keep stroking while varying the rhythm of your movements, the amount of pressure, and the type of touch. In order to not slip into other hand motions, you have to keep focused on the index finger's activity.

If you're completely concentrated, you will be able to stimulate yourself this way for a very long time.

7th Exercise

Erectile difficulties often arise when you already feel turned off before masturbating, or when you're not relaxed enough. Without external stimuli, the body is satisfied, and sexual urges reach a low point. In these times, sex is simply not very present in the mind. Such sexual apathy, which is often the result of previous sexual gratification, only fades away after a certain period of time, which is necessary to build up desire again.

But even in times of low desire, the brain reacts to involuntary stimuli. While there could be any kind of sexual fantasies that stimulate our senses indirectly, for the most part, stimulations come from the eyes and less frequently through our sense of smell. Though touch can be the ideal source of stimulation in other situations, it is often completely ineffective in moments like this. It can be completely normal and justified to let nature run its course. But on the other hand it's not unreasonable to want to reach that state of satisfaction again through intentional, deliberate stimulation.

The following exercise seeks simply to prove that it's possible—and in a very short period of time. It's enough to let thoughts and touch work together since each on its own likely wouldn't be enough. By bringing together certain touches and concentrated thoughts, a quite powerful stimulation can be reached.

With your right thumb and index finger, grab your still fully flaccid cock directly by the exposed cock head. Don't let your other fingers touch it. Grasp the base of your cock from above with your left thumb and index finger, positioning your index finger quite far below, between your balls.

During this exercise, you shouldn't watch yourself. Instead, keep your eyes shut, as you should do in most of the sitting exercises. (With standing exercises it's often more of a turn-on to look at your genitals from the start.)

Try to remember the hottest orgasm you've had recently. Concentrate entirely on the moment just before cumming.

Your left fingers should be pressed firmly, surrounding the base of the cock tightly. Your right fingers (from your other hand) should only touch it lightly. This variation in pressure is very important!

Now start making very slow, classic masturbation movements, letting your right hand only slide up and down half an inch each time. (No more.) Your foreskin should be pulled back entirely. Don't let your thumb slip; its movements should only touch the edge of the glans. At the same time, continue jerking strokes with your left thumb and index finger at the base of your cock.

The movements of your right fingers—which press your cock upwards—and your left fingers—which pull it down—need to be completely in sync. After only a short time, you'll notice a comfortable feeling, and have the urge to orgasm again. Now concentrate completely on how it felt the last time you had an extraordinary orgasm. Let your hand movements increase in pressure, but not in speed. You only need to continue these motions in opposite directions a little while longer, and you'll soon find yourself cumming ...

8th Exercise

Here's an exercise with an unusual kind of stimulation:

Lay your thumbs directly below the ridge of your glans on the top side of your cock, placing the next three fingers of each hand along the underside of the shaft with fingertips touching. Both pinkies should be touching the point where the base of the cock meets the balls. Now curve the fingers beneath your cock, one hand at a time. This movement results in a kind of tweaking that should be repeated by each hand about three times per second. This will lightly pinch the skin on your penis, and you will feel your shaft roll back and forth beneath your fingertips.

Now lift your balls lightly with your pinkies so that they will be stimulated by this motion as well. After about ten seconds of this very fast stimulation, which should be performed almost without pressure, simply move both of your thumbs slightly farther down the shaft without stopping the motion. Now only your index fingers will be touching the glans. Curve them alternately, exerting stronger pressure. The tweaking will increase, causing your glans to react accordingly. Now you have to position the tips of your index fingers at a steeper angle. In this new position they will push your glans downward as it grows larger, its ridge growing redder and touching the first joint of your index finger. The more your penis swells, the more clearly your thumbs will slide down to the middle of the top side of your cock, pressing more firmly as arousal increases. But since you've nearly got an erection, it will be difficult to hold your thumbs in the middle. Instead, put them back in their initial position, right below the ridge of the cock head. Now group your lower fingers in four pairs, fingertips across from one another along the shaft, middle fingers directly beneath your thumbs. With increasing speed and stronger pressure, perform the same tweaking as before, this time with all of your fingertips. In order to feel how pleasant this unusual feeling is, your thumbs need to touch your foreskin, which should lay behind the ridge of your cock head. By moving back and forth sideways, your thumbs will constantly roll along the ridge of the glans. Because your thumbs and other fingers are pulling at the foreskin together, your penis will move from side to side, and the cock head will seem to jump out of your fingers. This will lead to a pleasant erection.

Now let go of all your fingers except thumb and index, which should remain in the spot, with your thumbs a bit looser than before. Continue tweaking, increasing the pressure and growing faster, as long as your hands keep alternating. This stimulation can be carried out as long as you like without causing you to feel that you need to reach orgasm.

9th Exercise

Since lying down is typically a position for relaxation, it's perfectly normal that this position seems to be the least arousing. When fantasy dies down, weariness settles in quickly and ruins all good efforts.

Comfort causes tiredness, and not even sloth—mother of all vices—can find sufficient stimulation for sexual excesses while lying down.

In order to build up desire and sensuality, you've got to learn how to go about it first. So get naked and lie in bed.

Surveys have revealed that an appalling number of people go to bed in pajamas, jogging suits, and similar hiking apparel. In order to play with your body, to enjoy someone else's body, tenderness is essential. And tenderness, like sensuality, requires naked skin.

It's frightening how few people know the simple, pleasurable feeling of lying naked between the sheets or on the mattress, stretching out, rubbing their backs on the surface, letting their arms and legs slide around while stroking the fabric with their palms, curling up into a ball and then unrolling in order to crease the sheets with their fingertips and draping it in folds around their cock … the greatest luxury may be smooth, aromatic satin sheets.

And once one has gotten used to the pleasure of sleeping naked, nudity becomes a ritual and more than simply an unusual, refined pleasure: it becomes a gateway to the art of touching and feeling, which is intimately connected with sensuality. If nudity can be understood in this way, it's no longer a means but an end in itself.

For anyone who is still a stranger to this pleasure, this exercise simply consists in trying it out. How can anyone claim to have a fine-tuned sense of touch if they can't even manage to create harmony between their body and its immediate environment?

The bed is also there to help you learn to master your body. Stroke your whole body with the material, revel in the touch. Soon you'll ask yourself why you didn't enjoy these almost ecstatic moments much sooner. Let your hands slide over your body, aimlessly, everywhere. Stroke yourself again, without any desire beyond giving into your nakedness completely …

10th Exercise

This exercise does not claim to be effective for everyone. But it will give many men a chance to discover their own bodies. For many men, the idea that they have other erogenous zones besides their genitalia is uncomfortable. They often believe that only women know such varied sensations. But both men and women share the same nerve endings in their skin. There are countless other erogenous zones spread out over the entire body, and of course each person feels them differently. As a whole, the skin is unusual in that it encompasses the broadest spectrums of possible sensations: from unbelievable insensitivity all the way to the greatest over-sensitivity.

In this exercise, you are strongly urged to really get to know your own body and awaken your sensibility. It's entirely possible to achieve an erection without touching your penis at all. It can be enough to stroke your erogenous zones with your hands and fingers. Lay your flaccid cock on your torso and spread your legs slightly. Then close your eyes and relax completely.

Now you can start by touching your torso gently. Stroke with your fingers slowly up to your chest. Your fingertips should vibrate slightly, barely touching your skin. Slide up and down multiple times. With similar touches, stimulate your nipples as well.

Move your hand away and then let it wander back to your nipples. They will grow hard as a first wave of pleasure spreads throughout your upper body. Now you can touch them with your thumbs, arousing them further. Wet a finger with spit and run it over your entire upper body, your stomach, your thighs, and back to your chest. Rub your butt against the sheets, spread your legs a bit wider, bend your legs, and lift your pelvis.

Keep wandering over your body with your fingers. Your touches should be at light at times, and at other times stronger, harder. You can also bring your fingernails into play. But your hands should keep coming back to your nipples and you should keep wetting your fingertips.

Slowly, your cock will begin to get hard. Don't touch it. Simply stroke your whole lower body. Spread your thighs apart again and then pull them back to your body, tensing your pelvic muscles. Now, with your legs pulled in, press your upper thighs together tightly, then let your legs slip down again until they're stretched out straight. Now your balls will be caught between your thighs, pulled lower each time.

Your cock will become erect. Continue by lifting your thighs, pressing your buttocks together, and moving back and forth. You can repeat all of the stimulations described before. But don't forget to keep your nipples moist and to press your buttocks together …

11th Exercise

This exercise repeats some of the previous types of stimulation, but this time in more precise and refined ways. For someone with sensitive nipples, these touches are hot enough already. But in order to really enjoy them—and above all to be able to continue them for a longer period of time—you have to work with your head. Without masturbating—without even using your hands—it's possible not only to achieve an astounding erection, but to actually drive arousal all the way to orgasm!

In contrast with the previous exercise, during which the stimulation was mostly directed on your shifting body, the entire preparation for erection in this exercise concentrates solely on two points—while the body remains completely motionless!

Stretched out very straight on the bed, pull your balls down and capture them between your thighs, thus tensing the skin on your cock, which you should lay on your torso. Your thighs should be next to one another without pressing too tightly together.

From this point on you should not move. Close your eyes. Concentrate very hard. Soon you will feel erotic sensations. Then stimulate your nipples by twisting and tweaking them between your thumb and index finger. Lift your pelvis lightly and tense

41

the muscles in your chest, then press your butt firmly to the bed and hold your breath. As soon as your nipples grow hard, you should begin to pull down on them a bit. Now moisten them with spit and stroke around the nipple area with your middle fingers. Run your fingernails over the tips of your nipples. These motions should always be performed alternately, to let the sensations run into one another smoothly. Then pull your stomach in and tense your butt jerkily.

Your feet will touch. Now tense your thigh muscles. Your thighs shouldn't slip at all when you do this; just tense them strongly so that the muscles move slightly upwards. Then relax your thighs by pressing your knees together and spreading your butt cheeks. Your pelvis will lift slightly, while your butt will press deeper into the bed.

These movements should be barely visible; they are inner stimulations. Repeat them in a calm, regular rhythm, concentrating entirely on the sensations you feel.

Your cock will swell. Don't stop stimulating your nipples, and continue arousing your cock with the movement of your lower body, all the while holding your thighs tight together. Now when you tense your butt cheeks, your legs will seem to grow longer. As soon as you relax your buttocks and press them into the bed, your knees will lift lightly. All of these movements come primarily from the tensing and relaxation of the pelvic muscles, without the radius of motion exceeding a centimeter or two. It's not necessary to give way to sexual fantasies. The motion you're performing is like a regular, slow repetition of the forwards and backwards motion while fucking.

This whole time, you should continue stimulating your nipples. With one hand, you can pull the skin on your ball sack further down.

Stretch your legs out completely and tense your thigh muscles, causing them to rub together. This will increase the stimulation of your cock, which will continue to grow harder. Don't forget your nipples, which you can grab more firmly now. Concentrate entirely on what you are feeling, and keep your eyes closed.

Now you can cross your legs. Your cock will grow stiffer, increasing the feeling of pleasure. From this moment on, your pelvic motions can be more marked. If you continue, you can even cum this way.

12ᵗʰ Exercise

This exercise is also about achieving an erection. But this time we'll only focus on the base of the cock. You have to be very relaxed and certain that no one will disturb you. It's very important that all the preparations are carried out for this intimate little ritual. Make sure you have comfortable, soft lighting and appropriate lighting as every sense—not just touch—should play a role. Eroticism requires a comfortable environment. Desire can only be reached with care and time, and nothing is more of a turn-off than being in a hurry.

This exercise is no exception. The beginning stages of this stimulation might seem boring to you, but you will gradually realize that the relative slowness with which arousal is built up results in quite a special feeling. Don't throw in the towel after two or three minutes. This takes stamina.

Stretch yourself out, fully relaxed, with your legs slightly spread. Place your thumbs across from one another on the top side of your cock, right at the base—at the point where your pubic hair is already beginning. Your cock should rest on the thumbs, while the shaft should rest on your torso, pointed in the direction of your head.

44

Now press your middle finger firmly against the underside of the base of your cock, left and right of your balls. Your index fingers should also be placed right on the base, on either side of the axis where the balls begin. They should be positioned firmly as well. Your foreskin must be pulled back from the glans. Your fingers should form a ring around the base of your cock, as low as possible.

This is how you begin:

Without changing their position, slowly move your index fingers toward your middle fingers, catching a bit of the skin from your ball sack. At the same time, your fingers should dig horizontally into the base of your cock. Press your thumbs tightly against the top side, while your index fingers (laid flat) prolong stimulation.

All of these movements should be slow and thorough. Your cock should touch neither your torso nor your fingers. Pay attention to the movements of your index fingers. Before long you'll feel as though the base of your cock were stuck in a wrench. Tense your thighs without closing them. Continue the exercise by alternately performing the following stimulation with your fingers: push your hands further down about a centimeter without relaxing your firm grip on the cock base.

Your cock will increase in size—more in thickness than in length—because the skin is very tight. Don't move your fingers any more. Simply press your thumbs down harder against the top side. Keep your hands pressed flat into your crotch. From now on you can gradually increase the speed of the motion.

13th Exercise

The point of this exercise is to reach a certain level of arousal—to achieve an erection—without using your hands.

It's not about pretending you don't have hands, or reaching your goal purely through the power of thoughts. The cock doesn't act on command. It needs to be at least indirectly stimulated by the hands occupying themselves with other parts of the body, namely the secondary erogenous zones—above all the nipples and the anus.

Start this exercise by simply lying flat on your back with your left leg stretched out and your right leg crossed over it, causing your cock to be wedged between your thighs at its base. With the foreskin pulled back, the glans should poke out from between the thighs. Lean on your left elbow, keeping your upper body at a 45-degree angle with the bed. Through the pressure on the shaft, your glans will grow a darker color fairly quickly. Without moving your left leg, push your right knee up again. Your thighs shouldn't separate while doing this. Your pelvic muscles will be tensed again, placing massive pressure on your penis, which is now wedged in on all sides.

While you're stretching your knee, pull your stomach in to

release the pressure from that side. As soon as you lead your thighs back to their beginning position, your right ass cheek will automatically slip backwards, arching your back, and your cock will seem to disappear between the thighs.

Every time your thrust your knee forward and then back down, it's necessary to press your thighs firmly together.

Now you can increase the feeling of pleasure by stimulating your nipples with your fingers. Moisten your middle finger and let it stroke the areola, softly and quickly at first, then firmer and more slowly. Pinch them with your fingernails as well. The movement of your hips can now grow faster. If you look at your cock head while doing this it will be even more of a turn-on. The color of the glans is now getting darker. Soon you will only wish one thing: to keep going for a long time, to create a pleasurable feeling that you control. You won't even feel the need to cum. This feeling is distinctly strong and steady. You won't feel like masturbating normally, and you're not going to cum this way.

If you enjoy stimulating your anus, you can do that with your right hand now, while the left continues arousing your left nipple.

The intensity of arousal can be changed by letting yourself fall on your back, while your legs remain in the same position. The motions will be more marked now, and your cock will be pressed together even more at its base. You can also switch sides and then return back to your initial position. The goal is very pleasant arousal …

14th Exercise

On first glance, this exercise won't exactly seem simple to you, since the stimulation involved intentionally leaves out the sensitive zones of the body.

In fact, neither your balls nor the base or head of your cock will be touching your hands—only the shaft.

It's important not to forget that the shaft also reacts immediately to touch, and that it plays a role not only in masturbation but in sucking and fucking. However, with all those methods of stimulation, the glans is of course the extension of the shaft, and that's where we feel the nicest sensations. That's why orgasm happens after a relatively short period of time, almost always too soon.

Bizarrely, isolated stimulation of the glans or shaft doesn't lead to an enormous desire to cum right away. If each form of arousal is activated separately from the other, it's no problem to stay in control for much longer—assuming you don't give into the urge to get to the end quickly. After all, it's only normal to not want to hold back. If you're feeling good, you will just want to feel even better. That's why, even during foreplay, there's often such a rush.

Work hard to maintain your arousal on the plateau between

initial "lack of desire" and orgasm. If you keep yourself in this state of limbo, you won't end up ejaculating prematurely, and you will thus be able to enjoy the whole depth of pleasure—a state which is only increased by drawing it out. Just lay down on your back, your legs stretched out next to one another, touching lightly. Your balls should hang down normally—without any pressure—between your thighs.

Your cock should rest on your torso. Lay your thumbs down across from one another beneath the top side of the cock, while the next three fingers of each hand should be placed on the upwards-facing underside. The pinkies are spread away from the other fingers, touching the base of the cock on the left and right. They should merely be resting there, without taking part in the stimulation. Now begin to press the shaft against the fingers above it, which will provide resistance to this motion. Press very slowly and evenly, making sure that your thumbs are touching the middle of the shaft. At first, the pressure should be light. Keep this rhythm for about a minute, concentrating completely on your cock. Gradually you'll feel it getting harder. But don't move faster. You should go slower, but press harder. And each time, your thumbs should push deeper into the shaft. The pressure won't be constant, but instead will rise gradually. At the end of each movement, the pressure should be at its highest.

Your cock will get hard now, and at this point your other fingers should start directly stimulating it.

Since your thumbs are at the same height as your middle and ring fingers, your index fingers will be higher up. Use them to carry out a movement similar to the one you're making with your thumbs. While you do this, your thumbs shouldn't stop applying pressure. At this point all four fingers will be pushing together, making the pressure more distinct.

Now erection is reached. Make sure that your finger position doesn't change at all throughout the exercise.

By the end, your middle and pinky fingers should also be pushing more firmly, making your cock even harder.

15ᵗʰ Exercise

This exercise is particularly suited for getting an erection again when you've already cum in the past one or two hours.

Even if your cock is completely disinterested, and it seems not even the motions of classical masturbation would help, the motion you'll discover here can work miracles …

But to repeat: it's not enough for the proper movement to be carried out; it needs to be carried out at the right moment. If you're not precise, this exercise will turn you off completely. Only when you've repeated the motions described here multiple times, or tailored them exactly to your needs, will you reach the necessary precision.

Lie down, spread your legs a little, and grasp your flaccid cock from below with left thumb and index finger. Press your balls lightly down and to the side with the three other fingers of your left hand. Your penis will be lying in your crotch, pointed slightly to the right. The glans must be freed from the foreskin. Lay your right thumb and index finger against the top side of your cock, almost forming a ring around the ridge of the glans. Hold your other three fingers against the shaft, pointing towards the base of the cock, where they will touch the left thumb and index finger.

Your middle finger will lay right against the shaft, with the pinky and index finger left and right of it.

Now you can begin.

Press with your left fingers while your right fingers lean lightly against your cock. Your right wrist needs to be very flexible. Your elbows should be leaning on the bed next to your thighs. Instead of moving your arms, you will only be moving your wrist. As fast as you can, make vibrating motions with your wrist, turning about an eighth of a circle. This movement isn't strenuous at all. Just make sure to be relaxed and avoid any cramps. These fast, very small turning motions will seem to electrify your cock, which is only being touched by your right fingertips while your left thumb and index finger hold its base. Even after a few seconds, your cock will begin to expand. Now you can press your right thumb and index finger more firmly and then release again.

Maintain the same speed with your right wrist, then follow a slower motion for a few seconds. Your right thumb and index finger will move away from the underside of the glans. Lay them along your cock. Continue the vibrations, going faster then slower, finding your way back to the first speed, while your left hand pulls at your balls. Your cock will get increasingly larger but must stay trapped by your right hand. Soon you will be forced to slide your right fingers further up from the base of the cock until you've nearly reached the point of coming (again).

Extended Masturbation

This chapter is divided into two parts: the first is about dry masturbation, and the second covers masturbating with lube.

Though the movements in the various exercises of both parts may be similar, they are carried out in quite different ways. A lubed-up cock is more sensitive because it's in the same state as it is while fucking, which is more difficult to control. For most men, it's barely possible not to become weak; willpower is normally not strong enough to hold back lust.

For this reason, it's not immediately possible for most men in that situation to build up an inner block and shut out part of their sensations by restricting fundamental arousal to the physical level. It's got to be worked on, and the best way is through gradually built-up exercises towards controlled dry masturbation, which you should follow as closely as possible.

This extended masturbation uses motions that make it pretty easy to hold back ejaculation.

The most important rule for reaching full control over orgasm is to maintain a constant stimulating motion rather than giving in to the quite normal urge to use typical masturbating and fucking movements which will make you cum too quickly.

Keep your movement the same throughout the course of the exercise. This also applies for speed and pressure, though depending on your individual sensitivities there may be variations. But one thing should be clear: the longer your arousal lasts, the stronger your pleasure and orgasm will be!

What's more important is the fact that you can experience long lasting and repeated states of arousal without needing to have an orgasm. Even if ejaculation seems necessary in order to resolve normal sexual tensions, it's not unavoidable.

Even on a purely physical level, diverse stimulations and delayed orgasm can increase sexual tension so much that a maximal rush of blood to the penis is reached, which—when the tension is released—will lead to a truly divine orgasm. Simply because the phase where pleasure climbs is usually too short, men often have trouble distinguishing between ejaculation and orgasm.

This is so normal for most men that many believe orgasm occurs when ejaculation happens—or that ejaculation and orgasm are the same thing.

Equating the two might be accurate on a visual level. But otherwise it's not right. One thing all men share is the complaint that the phase before ejaculation is too short. All this means is that while ejaculation is part of the pleasure, it's the orgasm that's the absolute climax of the pleasurable sensation. At the same time, it's also the point of no return.

Men who are "lucky" enough to be able to hold off longer will always assure you that it's better before orgasm than afterwards.

There's also an unmistakable sign for lack of intensity in arousal when it comes to men who mistake ejaculation for orgasm: the lack of pre-cum, which normally appears a while before orgasm.

Pre-cum is simply a transparent, slightly sticky fluid—unrelated to sperm—which sometimes comes out of a flaccid penis, usually in its erect state. It functions as your body's own lube. As arousal increases, more of this newly produced liquid flows out, showing your contentment. Premature ejaculation can also occur when the glans is completely dry.

If you're a man who frequently cums too quickly, you should follow the following exercises exactly. It won't always be simple—at times you will give into the usual reflexes and make that decisive movement beyond which there's no return. If this happens, there's no need to get upset; instead you should resolve to hold out longer the next time.

Many of the following exercises avoid the classical masturbation hand grips—which are mostly too arousing to be sustained for a longer period of time, and which make it impossible to really make progress. Some of them use refined versions of the motions and stimulations from the previous exercises.

Nevertheless you will quickly be able to determine that these grips will also let you reach orgasm if you want them to.

Remind yourself that if you persevere, you will be doubly rewarded: your pleasure while masturbating will be absolutely extraordinary. And when it comes to fucking, you will reach a perfect control of ejaculation.

Don't let too much time pass between the individual exercises. In order to enjoy them and not lose interest, you should try them out shortly one after another—otherwise you're likely to fall back into your habits.

But if you notice that you're not in form one day or just not in the mood, it's better to put it off to another day. On the other hand, sometimes you don't work up an appetite until you actually go to eat …

When you're trying out these exercises—which are placed in a random order and contain something for everyone—you can select an order of increasing difficulty for yourself.

Extended Masturbation without Lube

1st Exercise

Sit on the edge of your chair, trapping your balls between your thighs, which should be gently pressed together. Start the stimulation as follows: grasp your cock beneath the exposed glans with the fingers of your right hand, while placing your thumb on top of your cock.

Two of the fingers of your left hand will help you by being positioned at the base of the cock—your index finger on the right and your thumb on the left, which should be bent so your fingernail is touching the penis.

It's better if you leave your legs slightly bent. Your back should stay very straight.

Press your cock with your two left-hand fingers, pulling it lightly downwards. With the fingers of your right hand, support the glans and make the classic up-and-down stroke, though gently. Rather than sliding your fingers along the shaft, keep them firmly anchored underneath the glans. This will stretch your cock and make it gradually larger. At the same time, exert an even pressure on the base of your cock with the fingers of your left hand.

Repeat this slow masturbating movement about four or five times a second. Each time you've reached the top of the stroke, press harder with your fingers than when your hand comes back down. Now you should nearly have an erection and can increase your speed. Both your left-hand fingers dig deeper into the base of the cock with each stroke—every time the fingers of your right hand pull your cock upwards.

Combining these two movements will markedly increase your sensations. Now you will reach the point where you feel the greatest urge to satisfy yourself quickly in the typical way. You have to resist this urge, since the goal of this exercise is to maintain arousal as long as possible, which will fill your cock and glans with more blood.

Let yourself simply fall against the armrest of the chair, without moving your buttocks or spreading your thighs. This simple change of position will make your cock even harder. The glans will swell. You will get faster and faster, which means you will have to slightly change the motion soon, because the pressing of your thumb will otherwise become nearly painful.

With your right wrist, carry out light horizontal vibrations, which you should vary by moving up and down. This will cause you to feel a tingling that comes in waves and runs from your butt down to your knees over the outside of your thighs.

Now you will reach the phase where you can maintain this feeling of pleasure as long as you want and simply enjoy the strokes without feeling the need to cum.

Close your left fingers into a ring and slide them softly along the whole length of your shaft, pressing more firmly when you move from bottom to top. At the same time, your right hand continues its vibrations.

You will feel a greater sensation of pleasure, but simultaneously a kind of excitement. It will almost seem to you as if you are approaching ejaculation.

Simply stop all your strokes for half a minute. Leave your hands in the same position. Close your eyes and relax. Breathe in deeply. Then keep going with the movements from before, but stronger and faster. If you think you're getting close to ejaculating again, just stop everything again—hold your breath even—and calm down again.

You will likely see pre-cum at the tip of your cock, a sign of an extreme level of arousal that comes before ejaculation. Take your hands off your cock and don't even touch yourself for about a minute. If your erection subsides a bit, you can continue. It will take a few seconds before your erection is as strong as it was before.

Your left hand should now fully close around your cock. Keep masturbating with the left hand, while the three fingers of your right hand lie directly beneath the cock head, not touching each other. From then on, you can "hold out" quite a while, since this stimulation can be continued for longer periods of time without the urge to ejaculate becoming too strong. As soon as you feel this urge, stop again by pressing your cock tightly: pre-cum will soon flow more strongly and cover your glans. This is good, since it shows that you can control yourself even though you're even more aroused.

After two or three minutes, simply continue with classical self-gratification—but only with your left hand. While you're doing this, I recommend short movements with middle-strong pressure.

Stay very slow, and keep the same rhythm. With your back still leaning and very relaxed, you can now stretch out your legs, spreading your thighs rather than pressing them together, leaving your balls free. Concentrate fully on the pleasure slowly spreading through you. You won't feel like coming anymore. You'll only want one thing: to keep going …

But you should follow this advice: you have to be strong enough to allow yourself a pause of at least fifteen minutes, letting your erection completely subside. This long phase of rest is absolutely necessary in order for arousal to disappear completely. After this pause, you can continue with your stimulation. After a short period of time, your erection will come back, even though you're only working very slowly with your left hand. Lay your forearm on the armrest or on your upper thigh to keep from making your movements too large. This is very important because it restricts your wrist's freedom of motion. Also make sure that your fingers don't stroke over the ridge of the glans. Your back-and-forth motions should stop directly beneath the glans.

A third cautionary procedure: while this arousal grows, you will tense your buttocks without noticing it. Your whole body will be under a storm because of your arousal, which will cause you to reach a climax quickly. Relax your ass cheeks and your legs; concentrate entirely on your slow, firm-yet-gentle—and above all, steady—hand motion.

You must succeed in thinking of your penis separately from the rest of your body: so stay loose, even though your cock is totally hard!

As soon as you've started pleasuring yourself again, close your eyes in order to concentrate better. If you've followed all of the previous instructions correctly, you will soon reach an ideal state of balance that you can hold for a long time: your cock is hard, and you can continue your very even hand motion without feeling the urge to cum.

From time to time you can increase the sexual tension by observing yourself. You should focus solely on your cock head while pressing your ass cheeks together and tensing the muscles in your legs. This combination will cause a sudden spike in pleasure.

Continue stroking until you feel ejaculation approaching—a tingling sensation in your lower back, shudders of pleasure in your upper thighs—then stop right away! Close your eyes, keep your hand grasped around your cock. Wait two or three seconds before continuing.

This time you'll be able to continue quite a while without stopping, under the condition that you keep your eyes closed and relax your pelvic muscles. At this point, you won't be able to ejaculate involuntarily. Now you will only cum when you really want to. You'll feel dizzy, entirely filled by a slightly numb and prickling sensation of pleasure. If you want to, you can maintain this state for another hour!

2nd Exercise

Again you're sitting, but this time far back in your seat. This time you will stimulate your cock with a stroke almost identical to what you will use as preparation for prolonged masturbation.

Your posture needs to be relatively relaxed, your thighs lightly spread apart, your legs stretched out. Focus your eyes on your cock.

First, close your left hand around your ball sack, forming your fingers nearly into a fist just beneath the base of the cock.

With your right hand, pull your foreskin back. You'll only reach an erection with the help of your thumbs and index fingers, which are positioned opposite one another. Both fingers rest directly beneath the glans without pushing down. Next, your left hand joins the action while both right-hand fingers slide back and forward. Don't do anything but these simple motions. The warmth that will rush to your balls will quickly flow into your cock as well, which—with the help of your finger movements—will expand in an astoundingly short period of time.

If you don't perceive any change after a few seconds, don't jump the gun. It won't help to be impatient. Your erection needs to result from this motion, because you're going to stimulate yourself with the same stroke afterwards, which will make your pleasure last even longer.

Any other stimulation would make it impossible for you to hold out longer later. Just focus on the two fingers around your glans. Let your thumb and index finger give subtle strokes, and you will find that this is enough to lead to a visible change.

Don't stop this motion. Instead, expand your radius of action. It should actually be impossible not to get an erection after one or two minutes.

The longer you continue, the more the skin on your cock will be stretched, giving your right fingers much narrower contact with the sensitive spot they're touching.

Without easing off, you can now keep going like this for many minutes with the same stamina. Your left thumb and index finger should push deeper and deeper into the base of your cock, while you tense your lower stomach muscles. Now you should feel your anus pulling together as you reach erection.

Afterwards, your goal will be to increase your still diffused pleasure without falling back into classical masturbation.

Now pull your cock upwards as strongly as possible while simultaneously increasing the pressure at the base. If you keep doing this long enough, you will only feel like continuing your pleasure in this manner. Now you can alternate short up-and-down strokes with these longer ones, which should be just as quick without changing the position of your fingers on your cock.

In the next few minutes, your cock will reach a state of absolute hardness. Your glans will grow dark red. This is the right moment to change the stimulation fundamentally.

Lay your forearm comfortably on the armrest. This will be necessary, since the stroke you're going to use now demands this kind of support.

Place your fingers around the glans without touching it. Don't put any pressure on it—this stroke is only possible at this speed if your fingers stay open. The movement originates in the wrist, a short and very quick vibration. This tapping should touch the ridge of your glans, while your thumb lies on top of your cock with your other fingers beneath it.

At the same time, hold your balls tight in your left hand, pumping them together.

Next close your right-hand fingers firmly around your cock head, pulling upwards—as if you wanted to separate it from the rest of your cock. Repeat this pulling about 20 times. It will noticeably increase the blood flow to your glans. Then take up the previous motion again, alternating it with the new one. Your arousal will increase, causing a prickling sensation throughout your crotch area.

Next, keep making those vibration motions without letting go of the head of your cock: the feeling will grow more intense. A kind of wave will seem to emanate from your glans, filling your entire cock down to the balls. Your left-hand fingers should now let go of your balls and grasp the root of your shaft. With thumb, index, and middle finger, start massaging in this position with short, firm gestures, sending this wave back to the head.

These alternating movements will cause a sensation of half-pleasure, half-irritation, which you will sometimes want to maintain and other times not. If you keep going for a long time, you will overcome the feeling of irritation and reach a phase of intense ecstasy. Continue varying all of these movements. After a while, depending on the individual, your arousal will suddenly grow strong, and pre-cum will begin to flow. At this point, you could cum soon ...

Stop right away. Don't move any more. Close your eyes and don't think of anything but your breath, which should be even and deep. This will cause you to calm down. In a few seconds, the tension will subside and you will be able to think clearly again.

It's normal for your erection to subside a bit, since your arousal has left the phase where you felt the need to cum. Now you can masturbate as long as you like, in a way you wouldn't have been able to imagine beforehand. Your stimulation has aroused your glans and the blood is waiting to be reactivated.

From now on you can pleasure yourself as follows:

With your left hand, stroke your shaft slowly and with pleasure, pulling the skin up and down without touching the highly sensitized glans. Do this very slowly. Then make the same stroke with your right hand, very quickly this time. After about 20 such movements, change hands again. With this varying use of your hands, you can markedly extend your pleasure and masturbation.

Because of the prolonged stimulation that began this exercise, you can now control your semen from rising much more easily.

Even if you feel you're about to cum, you can keep going for a few seconds and then stop at the right moment by decreasing your pressure and speed by half. Immediately, the urge to ejaculate will go away. Then you can start from the beginning, this time without any difficulty. Everything is under your control.

It can be even more beneficial to stop this exercise without ejaculating.

3rd Exercise

Adopt the same position as before, but leave your legs some-what looser this time. This exercise is particularly arousing, caus-ing particularly intense sensations. What's interesting about this exercise is that it's entirely focused on the spot just below the ridge of the cock head, which is the only spot you will touch. What's even more interesting is that from the beginning of the exercise down to potential ejaculation, the same fingers (or even just fin-gertips) are carrying out the strokes. Two or three simple changes in motion can be enough to vary your pleasure quite effectively.

Spread your upper thighs wide, letting your balls hanging free, unhindered. Watch what your hands are doing. In this exercise, you can keep your eyes open from beginning to end without run-ning the risk of ejaculating too early. Don't get irritated if this exercise seems boring to you. If you keep at it, you won't regret it.

Pull your foreskin back from the head of your cock, leaving it just beneath the ridge of the glans in a bulge. Now lay both thumbs on top of this bulge and put both index fingers beneath it, letting your fingertips touch. Now let time work for you.

With your fingers, make an even sliding motion: when your thumbs slide upward, your index fingers should slide downward.

For the first minute, it will seem like nothing is happening. But don't stop—the first changes will soon become apparent. Very gradually, your cock will swell. Make sure that your index fingers pull more clearly downward, while your thumbs just push the foreskin over the ridge of the glans without covering it. This is important, since stimulation can only be built up effectively at this spot.

From time to time you should return your fingers to their original spot, since they will have the tendency to drift. This is particularly important for the thumbs, which you should not let slide down the cock. Their radius of motion should remain extremely small.

As your cock gets harder, carry out the previously described stroke even faster, while pressing down more firmly with your thumbs. This will lengthen your cock and lead to erection. Maintain this rhythm for a few minutes until your glans swells. Now you will feel the sensations more clearly. And at this time you should allow your cock a new form of pleasure …

Grasp your bulging foreskin on both sides of the shaft with your index fingers and thumbs, pinching it together lightly. While you pull on the skin, use your left-hand fingers to press your shaft into your right-hand fingers, opening the fingers of your right hand slightly and then closing them again, pushing the shaft back between the fingers of your left hand.

In order for this sensation to be effective, your movements need to be pretty fast to start with, and then need to grow even quicker. It's quite simple if you don't go too fast, but will grow more difficult as you get faster. Your hands need to work fully in sync.

Next, start up the previous motions again, which should now feel quite differently due to the increased tension in your cock. Because of your hard-on, the skin will be pulled down towards the base of your cock. The movements of your thumbs will need to be even shorter, pushing your cock head upwards at the ridge. Your thumbs need to be right in the middle, pressed firmly, while both index fingers are a bit further down on the underside, pulling the frenulum as far down as possible with each motion.

Arousal will increase, your glans will swell and grow dark. An intense feeling of pleasure will set in.

Now start the horizontal pinching movements again—always just below the glans, as if you wanted to separate it from the rest of the cock. It will get particularly hard now.

Vary both motions for several minutes, increasing the blood flow and strengthening your erection.

Now add a third variant to the two basic motions, pushing all four fingers together up and down: while your right thumb and index finger slide up, slide your left thumb and index finger down. Increase both speed and pressure. As this motion becomes quicker, it will gradually become circular, strengthening arousal.

From now on you can alternate all three motions however you like. Arousal will spread to your ass cheeks, which will grow tense, pressing your thighs up. Your legs will tense as well, and you will have a perfect erection. You will have reached the stage where you just want to grab hold of your cock and masturbate. There's nothing wrong with doing this if you feel like it. But remember that you can delay your ejaculation more if you can manage to keep your arousal at a higher plateau for longer. This has advantages, both for sustained masturbation and for fucking.

After a few minutes, your stamina will be rewarded: you will feel a very intensive feeling of contentment that makes you simply feel like continuing. You've passed the dangerous phase: your glans is full of blood, making it sensitized. But what's more important is that some drops of pre-cum will likely be appearing at your cock tip, displaying intense pleasure and proximity to ejaculation.

But there's no need to stop. Simply diminish pressure and speed; this will be enough to release some sexual tension. You don't even need to look away. Now you will reach a phase where you can maintain the same state as long as you like. This feeling is like a penetrating wave of pleasure that doesn't let up. From this point on you have three possibilities: you can stop this prolonged stimulation by going over to the usual methods of self-stimulation; you can simply stop without feeling the need to ejaculate—and without being unsatisfied because of it; or you can just continue with these strokes. If you decide to do that, you will notice that the extreme pleasure that comes before orgasm has a very different quality than it does with "traditional" masturbation.

4th Exercise

Here's an exercise for a long-lasting, quite astounding stimulation. Sit back relaxed and simply start to pleasure yourself with one of the erection-building exercises.

As soon as your cock is half hard, form a ring with your right thumb and index finger directly beneath the ridge of the glans. Pull on your balls with your left hand. Start masturbating in the classical way, from top to bottom, without allowing the ring at the ridge of your glans to slip.

By repeatedly hitting the ridge of the glans, you will stretch your cock. This is the same procedure outlined the first part of this chapter, although here your fingers are positioned differently. The ring should slip at most one or two centimeters. It's important that your foreskin doesn't slip over the glans with each stroke. Your penis will be stretched, and each of these short movements ends with a stroke against the ridge of your cock head, which will be nearly strangled and pushed upwards. Your erection will grow, and the first pleasurable feelings will start to spread.

From the start, your strokes should be slow and very even. With every upward stroke, close the ring a bit tighter and exert considerable pressure. Keep your other fingers open, without touching the penis. As soon as you feel stronger tension, close the ring even tighter, as if you wanted to squeeze your balls. Then stop for a bit—a few seconds are enough. Start again, but faster this time, making the ring a bit looser. After that you can go slower again while closing the ring tighter. Now stop stimulating your balls with your left hand. Just move your hand away and relax your arm. Only your right hand and the ring formed by your fingers will continue as before. Your erection should be quite pronounced. If you bend your legs, you can relax your thighs even more. Your glans will grow redder and larger. All you need now is to vary pressure and speed without changing the ring's radius of motion. As soon as you feel that you're about to cum, reduce the speed of your strokes to a minimum. This stimulation might be tantalizing enough to make you dizzy. From now on you can influence your level of sexual arousal, either strengthening or weakening it as you like: all you need to do is pull your fingers together as firmly as possible into a ring, leaving your legs relaxed, then stretch your legs out and release the pressure on your fingers a bit. Pre-cum will start to flow.

You have reached the so-called plateau phase, a period of sexual response that you can extend as long as you like.

In order to work up a desire to ejaculate only to interrupt it at the right moment, change up your pace.

Release your right-hand fingers from your cock, masturbating energetically along the whole length of the shaft with your left hand without covering the glans. You can keep doing this quite a long time before needing to stop again.

The way you've been stimulating yourself from the start of this exercise will now allow you full control. When you feel ejaculation coming, you can suppress it any time if you want to.

You will also notice that your erection has become quite solid and durable, so to speak. As proof, all you need to do is interrupt your hand motions—your erection will remain unchanged for quite a long time as the blood flow is perfect. Now you have to wait a while before your erection gradually subsides.

Keep masturbating with your left hand, this time letting your hand slide over the glans. The feeling of pleasure will return, a feeling that you now fully control.

The longer you continue, the dizzier you will feel, as if you're in a trance. Even if your cock were now to penetrate something, you would maintain full control over your ejaculation.

You can increase your arousal by alternating masturbation between your left and right hand. As soon as you feel the urge to be 'finished,' pull the ring of your thumb and index finger firmly together. Now you can even dominate an ejaculation that was on its way: press as strongly as if you wanted to squash your cock. If you relax your muscles at the same time, the danger will be over.

You can relax for a few minutes, or take your hands away – your penis will remain hard.

You've reached such an intense level of arousal that you will want to maintain it for a few minutes. Nothing is simpler: bend your legs or stretch them out while you keep pleasuring yourself. As long as you keep your eyes closed, you won't ejaculate. As soon as you stretch out your legs, relax your muscles, and look at your cock, you will feel ready to blow your load.

The decision is all yours. You will feel clearly in control: you can either stop now—without feeling any frustration—or you can decide to cum right away.

5th Exercise

This exercise for prolonged masturbation is particularly ideal if you've recently ejaculated.

It's interesting for two reasons: It brings you to erection very quickly, even if your cock was small and lackluster before. But above all, you can continue your self-gratification as long as you like without the slightest interruption.

The exercise is most beneficial if you're completely relaxed, with your back supported in a chair or sofa.

I'd like to mention a mistake that many men make: they try desperately to reanimate their fully flaccid penis with jerky back-and-forth strokes. This usually yields no results.

In these cases, it is much more effective to use a "vibration" rather than a stroke.

While seated, clamp your balls fully or partly between your thighs, which you should press together with your legs stretched out.

Position your thumbs and index fingers as supports, without pressing down, at the base of your cock. Your cock rests in your right hand, while your right fingers grasp it lengthwise from top to bottom. Your thumb should lie on the upper side of the cock.

Slightly bend your wrist. Your cock will lie lengthwise in your hand, parallel to your fingers, even if it's still small now.

With a quick shaking movement of your wrist, move your fingers faster and faster without grasping your cock: higher-speed vibrations arise, causing your cock to alternately beat against your thumb and your other fingers.

Even after a few seconds, you will feel the first results: your cock will grow somewhat larger. As it expands, don't stop. At the same time, stimulate the base of your cock with the fingers of your left hand using a rhythmic, not too strong pressure. Stretch your legs out completely. Tense all your muscles, your butt as well. Inevitably, your cock will reach a nearly-erect state.

Now position your right fingers differently, closing them just beneath the glans and continuing the vibrations as fast as you can without releasing your grip. These vibrations will affect the middle of your shaft above all, a movement somewhat similar to a rope spun from one side.

Now form the fingers of your left hand into a ring at the base of your cock, starting with short, rubbing motions that run up and down from the middle of your cock to the base. Close your left-hand fingers more and more around the base, rubbing more forcefully. After a few up-and-down gestures, close your entire left hand around the root of your cock.

Next, alternate these two techniques: vibrations with the right hand and massages with the left. Do this as long as you can continue producing the same kind of oscillation, and then change your grip: pull your cock lengthwise with slow, firm back-and-forth strokes. As soon as your left hand squeezes, your right hand pulls your cock upwards. Then alternate the two stimulations with your left hand, exerting pressure three or four times followed by more intense massages.

Soon you might feel like continuing in a different manner. Do it! The left hand's massage strokes will become typical masturbation strokes practically by themselves. At the same time, close your fingers more firmly around the head of your cock. Then let go completely. Continue your left hand's back-and-forth strokes without touching the glans. Press the cock shaft more firmly, slowing down your strokes even more.

Your legs have been pressed together since the beginning, but you can spread them slightly apart now, freeing your balls. It will feel as if you could keep going like this forever. You will feel horny without being overpowered by your desire. Relax your touch by opening your left hand a bit, all the while speeding up your strokes. After a few seconds you will feel ready to shoot your load.

Now relax all your muscles, slowing your strokes again with your hand closed firmly around the shaft. After a short pause, continue the fast up-and-down motions with your hand open. You will get horny again.

You can switch hands and continue with the other in a normal, even rhythm. Strangely enough, you have passed the critical phase without even noticing it.

Soon you will find yourself in a trance-like phase, only vaguely realizing that you're masturbating, as if your consciousness had been lulled to sleep. Your hand's gestures are hardly your own anymore and have become almost automatic. Next to sexual gratification, your most tangible feeling will certainly be pride. Pride because you've managed to get this far even if you wouldn't have thought you could before.

In order to reach that particularly intense state which sets in directly before ejaculation, you can continue the previously described exercises with your left hand. The fact is, it is ideal to carry them out with this hand, since you can increase your pleasure for a longer period of time than with your right, sustaining it as long as you like.

After long, firm masturbation—and after the desire to ejaculate has faded somewhat—you can gradually go faster again, opening your hand a little. These changes in rhythm should never be rushed. Always maintain continuity.

Finally you will reach the point where you were before, but slower this time, so that you have time to get used to it. This way, you will experience a kind of orgasm even before ejaculation.

It can be enough simply to divert your thoughts a bit. But if you want to cum, all you need to do is concentrate on your penis ...

6th Exercise

This exercise is particularly interesting for men who prefer a firm grip from the start.

Here it's all about using a slight variation of a classical masturbation stroke to bring a flaccid or tired cock to erection.

With natural arousal, it's normally unnecessary to support the penis by stimulating the balls. A penis that's "in the mood" doesn't need any extra help. Mostly, these extra touches will overwhelm one with pleasure, causing ejaculation to cum too soon.

But when the penis is fully flaccid it can be necessary to supplement your stimulations. Whether they should be gentle or firm depends on your own taste and current mood.

If you're already horny before starting to stimulate yourself, any caress or touch is welcome. In this case the objective is the opposite: to hold out as long as possible, rather than building tension in the quickest possible time span.

If you feel positive changes after some desired stimulation, you should definitely continue those stimulations rather than switching to a new kind of stimulation. Switching would slow down the process you've already begun, if not completely interrupt it.

This is how it goes.

For this exercise, remain standing; this position alone will play a part in your success.

Tense your leg muscles, as this will increase the effectiveness of your hand strokes. With your legs pressed together, you can squeeze your ass cheeks together more easily. The tension in these muscles will support your emerging erection.

With your left hand, grasp your balls while pressing your thumb and index finger on both sides of the base of your cock. Bending your thumb will make this much more effective. Both fingers will dig into the root of your cock, while the others will pull your ball sack down.

Position your right thumb on top of your cock. The glans shouldn't be entirely free, since the foreskin will need to fully glide over it later. Position your index and middle finger on the underside across from your thumb, right in the middle.

With these three fingers, begin a classic masturbating stroke. Avoid pressing too softly or too firmly. At the beginning, the fingers will stay in position, meaning they won't move over the surface, but instead will force the cock to stretch. The whole shaft will be pulled. At first, your strokes should be medium fast, as if you had already progressed to the middle of coitus. Your left hand will hold your ball sack and massage it. Continue pressing with your thumb and index finger. At equal intervals, tense your butt cheeks and relax them again. The rhythm of this movement should be slower than your masturbating rhythm. In the first seconds, all these efforts will seem to produce no effect. You just have to keep going without changing a single detail. As you're doing this, watch your cock.

After just a few seconds, at most a minute, a reaction will be automatic and your cock will grow. Now increase the pressure. Above all, the following detail is important: if your right fingers pull your cock longer, grasp more firmly. The movement can be like a thrust beating against your glans. The effect itself will be more interesting than your emerging erection. This stimulation will create a very pleasant feeling, but it can only work if the rhythm of your masturbation is very fast.

While your cock grows larger and larger, it will be more and more difficult to let your fingers rest in the proper position. Pull the skin back from the head of your cock. It would be too soon to start masturbating in a classical way now by pulling the skin back and forth over your glans and penis. Just change your grip, positioning your fingers a bit further down so your skin isn't stretched as much. Keep going the same way for a while – until you hit the barrier where other strokes become necessary.

Don't forget to keep massaging your ball sack with your left hand. Tense your legs, keeping your ass cheeks firm.

The persistence of three different stimulations will finally lead to erection, though the movement of your skin will become more difficult, almost painful. Don't let up yet. Your glans can be much more strongly aroused and full of blood. This will make it even simpler to extend masturbation.

When you finally let your three fingers slide over the surface of the cock, the feeling will be almost unpleasant. But you would actually prefer to keep going as before. The feeling won't stop. Now masturbate normally, quite firmly, with those three fingers alone. Don't grasp your cock with your entire hand. Only thumb, index, and middle finger will let you reach this overwhelming state, which you can then savor as long as you like.

You will feel a wave of contentment that seems to roll up your legs to your cock, only to roll back down. You would like to sustain this feeling of pleasure, and it won't be hard. If you tense your upper thighs now, you will ejaculate soon.

By shifting your weight off your legs and then spreading your relaxed legs a bit, the feeling of impending ejaculation will subside, or even disappear. You don't even need to stop pleasuring yourself. After a few seconds, stand back up on both legs. Let your left hand work on your balls with renewed energy. Whenever you feel you're about to shoot, change your position again.

After you've changed position three or few times, the urge will grow stronger. Remain in the relaxed position for more time. Make sure not to wait to change your position until it's too late!

If you're about to ejaculate, relax on your free leg and standing leg, tensing your ass cheeks. This will let you interrupt the impending ejaculation.

The first drops of pre-cum will appear at the tip of your cock.

Now you've passed the phase where you could ejaculate unintentionally. You can hold yourself back without needing to interrupt your masturbation—until you decide to cum.

7ᵗʰ Exercise

If you want sex, you should always give yourself time: Time to stroke your partner, time to love yourself. Time to masturbate.

True pleasure can only arise under this condition.

But it seems that only few men realize this. Why can't they even imagine anything better when it would be in their best interests?

Maybe it's because they always thought that sexual arousal, as soon as it is achieved, is too overwhelming to be controlled. That's why they take the simplest, shortest path. When it comes to this, men are hardly different from animals, since what's lacking here is not so much intelligence as willpower. Or if you like: his intelligence doesn't lead him to prove his willpower in these moments.

Only willpower could allow him to control his urges, channel them, and then submit to them only when he decides.

Expressed practically: The more a stimulation is maintained, the more the senses are aroused, your erection will also last longer, and ejaculation will be more overpowering. This exercise should prove this to you.

Follow the instructions exactly. This will help you learn to control your will as well.

From start to finish, you will be using practically the same stroke. Stand up with your legs and ass relaxed. If you're right-handed, your left hand will take care of business, except for the last few seconds when you feel like coming.

Position your fingers as follows:

Place your thumb on the top side, halfway between the middle of your cock and the ridge of the glans, which should be exposed. Place your other fingers next to one another, slightly spread, your index finger at the height of your frenulum, your pinky down below where the ball sack begins, pressing tightly. From the start, your fingers should sit quite firmly. Your four lower fingers should pull your skin as far down as possible, not moving otherwise. Just push your glans forward with your thumb, pressing firmly to let a bit of foreskin slip back over the ridge of the glans.

It's very pleasant to watch your cock throughout the exercise.

Keep making back-and-forth strokes with your thumb, beating slowly, regularly and clearly against the ridge of the glans. You will see that your glans changes color quite quickly, and that your cock grows larger as well.

If you have already half reached an erection, keep going, now moving your lower fingers as well—but in the opposite direction. Your thumbs and four other fingers will move in opposite directions, pulling the frenulum down while your thumb pushes your cock head up. Make sure that your finger movements don't become too simultaneous, since this would be too similar to classic masturbation. If you carry out these strokes the way I've described, you can keep them going for a long time without feeling the desire to ejaculate too soon.

If you notice the urge increasing, don't change your rhythm or pressure. Simply make smaller motions. It's also important here to look away. That will be enough. Your urge is back under control.

As soon as your erection is quite firm, pay close attention, since this motion can lead to ejaculation on its own.

The advantage of this finger position is that you can press quite firmly. If you feel you're about to cum, you just need to squeeze your cock, and your ejaculation will be controlled in a few seconds without the intensity of your erection subsiding.

As soon as you've gotten past this hurdle, you will notice that your erection is now durable. You can interrupt everything for ten seconds or more without your erection jumping ship. Alternate stimulation with pauses. Each time, the pleasure will be greater afterwards, though entirely controllable.

But you can increase your pleasure even more: Lay your lightly opened fingers down as if they were positioned on the trigger of a gun. Touch and pull the skin of your cock with your lower fingers, pushing it firmly downward. Press more strongly with your thumb, bending your penis to the right.

As with most of these stimulations, you will no longer necessarily feel the need to cum at the end of this exercise. Your feeling of horniness will be very intense. Even though you haven't ejaculated, you won't be dissatisfied or frustrated. It could even make you proud. On the other hand, you could just as well ejaculate, since you've more than proven to yourself that you can hold back as long as you like.

Since the period of arousal has been very long, your orgasm and ejaculation will be quite overwhelming.

Hold your hand in its first position and masturbate further with a radius of motion that is very small while remaining fast.

Two or three seconds will be enough.

If you want an even stronger ejaculation, you've got to use your right hand—but put it in the same position.

8ᵗʰ Exercise

This exercise is intended for men who generally cum too early—regardless of whether or not they have difficulties achieving an erection.

These men in particular must get to know their sexual sensitivities well in order to control their unexpected ejaculations.

Normally the assumption is that premature ejaculations only happen during fucking. When it comes to jerking off, this is rarely mentioned. In my opinion, the problem of premature ejaculation can be solved. And those men who masturbate in addition to fucking can prove this. Because masturbation can lead to "healing" here, as long as men with this problem can accept that self-gratification is not merely a back-up solution.

This exercise is doubly interesting:

On the one hand because you will stimulate yourself in a variety of ways, and on the other hand because they follow one another in a logical order, after a longer period of rest each time. At first, the stimulations will be short and the pauses long, then the relationship will reverse.

Stand up. For the whole exercise, keep your eyes fixed on what you're doing. This is necessary in order to balance visual arousal, which leads to the urge to cum soon, with your masturbating technique, delaying ejaculation.

If you're right-handed, start the stimulation with your left hand. Place your thumb, middle, and ring finger somewhat under the middle of your cock, closer to the torso. Your grip needs to be very light. Shake your cock up and down with quick squeezes. Since it's still soft, the upper half will flop clearly back and forth. Of course, your glans should be exposed.

Your penis will swell quicker than you expected. Don't stop now—keep up both the medium speed and light pressure.

Even if your cock is already half aroused, don't change anything. Just push harder with your thumb.

Keep this stimulation going as long as you can, since it will be the basic foundation to turn you away from premature ejaculation. First, since your glans is only indirectly stimulated, and second, because the part of your cock that you are touching is the least sensitive part. Additionally, you can maintain an erection with this stimulation for a long time, since it won't remind you of the classic up-and-down strokes.

When your cock is fully hard and you can't bend it with your shaking motion, slide your fingers lower towards its base. Here the motion will become much faster. Your thumb should press with twice as much force here as your fingers on the underside. Now your pinky will be positioned next to the other fingers. The shaking gesture will now very pronounced and almost nervous.

If you tend to have difficulties reaching erection, simply tense your ass cheeks firmly. That in itself will increase sexual tension. If you don't have those difficulties, concentrate instead on relaxing your butt.

Now you've achieved erection: your cock will wiggle back and forth, your glans will grow red. Continue this stimulation for at least fifteen minutes. But you don't have to worry about ejaculating. This stroke simply supports the flow of blood into the shaft of penis, but it won't cause you to blow your load. Then stop and give your cock a break for at least five minutes. As soon as this period is over, position your fingers exactly the same as before the interruption. Now your cock will be less hard. Simply start stimulating yourself the way you were before. Very quickly, your cock will reach the same state as before. Now counteract the pressure of your thumbs by exerting stronger pressure with your other fingers. Your cock has just reached solid erection again. Held tightly at the base on both sides, it will now swing counterclockwise in a wide circle.

Maintain this rhythm as long as you can. Then interrupt it again—only this time take a break for two minutes.

After this break, you will notice that your erection hasn't subsided as much as it did before. Renewed stimulation will also show an effect much faster. When your penis is hard again, change the position of your fingers on the underside of the shaft: Press them into the ball sack, pulling it downwards noticeably. Only your index fingers should now be surrounding the base of your penis.

From now on continue the same movement described above, making your strokes shorter and more restricted. Your foreskin should be pulled back completely; the feeling of pleasure in your cock should get stronger, and your glans will be maximally sensitized.

Continue this stimulation as long as possible. Even now, you don't need to worry about ejaculating. It won't just happen—and if it did, it wouldn't be premature any longer.

At this point in time, the urge might arise to masturbate in a classic manner. Don't give in to this desire. Instead, stop completely for 20 or 30 seconds. Your erection will stay firm—until the moment that you really want to cum.

9ᵗʰ Exercise

Of course it's easy to hold back ejaculation when your strokes aren't similar to "classic" masturbation. On the other hand, there are also techniques that use very similar hand motions.

The following exercise is dedicated to this time-tested hand grip.

This exercise is also performed while standing.

Men who tend to ejaculate prematurely should absolutely take breaks as they are described here, even if they get shorter as the exercise goes on. The most important point of this rather traditional exercise is to sustain arousal for as long as possible.

Any other previously mentioned methods can be used for help if needed: look at what you're doing or look away, relax your muscles or tense them, "work" your nipples or leave them alone.

This time, start stimulating yourself however you like, using your own method or one of the ones previously described in this book.

This exercise doesn't begin until you already have a solid erection and can feel the first waves of pleasure. This is the nicest phase—which is exactly why most men just rush here, instead of letting it last longer.

A tip for premature ejaculators: let go of your cock as soon as you feel you're about to cum! A second too late and it'll all be behind you!

After a self-determined break, start masturbating again with classic up-and-down strokes, just as if you hadn't taken a break at all. Don't forget that it's very important whether your ass cheeks are relaxed or tensed. Another piece of advice for the hasty: as soon as you feel a wave of more intense contentment, more distinct than before, have the willpower to interrupt yourself. And for everyone: think about how much more powerful your ejaculation will be the more you can keep your arousal in control.

Now is the most important phase, right before the point of no return. If your legs were touching before, spread them slightly, about a foot's width apart. Bend lightly forward. As you continue to masturbate, tense your pelvic muscles and push your butt back. But above all, make sure to push your penis downwards.

This time, it will seem like it's going to happen: you'll feel the tension rise suddenly—another two or three seconds and you'll cum!

Without stopping, carry out the following instructions:

Bend both knees about four inches, pull your stomach and buttocks in. Don't really tense your upper thighs while doing this; instead, support yourself on your legs, staying quite relaxed. Above all—and this is very important—hold your cock vertically, very close to your stomach. The feeling of impending ejaculation will fade immediately. Now you can keep going as you're far enough away from coming.

In order to reach the point just before ejaculation again, position yourself as before and repeat everything. Each time, the effectiveness of this exercise will astound you. You're playing with fire, but you don't ever have to interrupt your masturbation. Your desire is perfectly in control.

10th Exercise

Lying down is undoubtedly the most relaxed position. For this reason alone, it's possible to masturbate longer this way, extending the pleasurable period before ejaculation.

Because your body isn't moving, it can abstract away from the purely physical. In this state of relaxation, it's not so difficult to work up the willpower to stop at the right time. However, it is difficult to turn off your thoughts.

Lay back fully relaxed and spread your legs, which will make it easier to leave your leg and butt muscles relaxed. This position alone, and your nudity, should be enough to give you the beginnings of an erection without using any of the strokes described here. From this point on, the desire to cum is usually greater than the desire to prolong your pleasure. Which means would start with normal, rushed masturbation, which can last as little as a few seconds.

Of course you could just do this, and then repeat the whole thing in one or two hours. Who could blame you? But remember that the second time around, your pleasure would not be as strong as the first time. Even if it would last longer, its quality would be very different and your ejaculation would definitely be weaker.

It would be preferable if you had as much self-control the first time around as most men only have the second time around. This seems to be very difficult for many men.

It's also important to remember that you ejaculate faster if someone is masturbating you. This more intense sensation comes from your mind and is more psychological than physical, since you picture what is happening in your head.

For this reason, it's crucial to try these exercises out on yourself, getting to know your body before you can better savor and extend the greater pleasure of having someone else masturbate you.

Begin by pleasuring yourself in the classic manner. But before you feel any waves of pleasure run through, lay your right hand on top of your penis, directly on top of the glans, which you never rub directly: make quick strokes up and down, with your foreskin almost covering the glans. The ring formed by your index finger and thumb shouldn't slide further down than the ridge of the glans. If your hand moves upwards, the entire tip of your cock should disappear in your fist and be nearly fully grasped.

Now close your left hand over the bottom half of your cock, exerting strong, even pressure. If you make sure that your penis is horizontal, the position of your hands will feel like penetration.

In order to put a bit of a brake on your horniness, exert quite a lot of pressure with every stroke upwards towards the tip of your cock. But if you want to increase that feeling, make shorter up–and-down strokes restricted to the ridge of the glans, which should remain covered by your foreskin. The tip of your glans shouldn't poke out of your fist.

Besides these variations, you can explore the various possibilities that a change in speed allows: your upwards strokes should be very slow, and you can even slow down the whole up-and-down motion while making the short strokes very fast.

A change in pressure can also cause new sensations: use a firm grip when your hand is at the top, and a very light grip when it reaches the base of the glans.

If you feel yourself getting more aroused, you can loosen your left hand grip. Now only your left index finger and thumb are closed tightly around the base of your cock. This will bring the sensation down to a bearable level. If you feel like you're about to blow your load in spite of this technique, interrupt everything for a bit and curve your cock towards your stomach. The urge to ejaculate will subside.

By this time your erection will be very solid and the longer you masturbate, the more intensely blood will flow to the shaft.

Your mind can play a decisive role in this. As soon as you've avoided the point of no return and left it behind you, you can extend this plateau phase almost endlessly—so long as you can separate mind and body. Concretely, this means that your hand should pleasure you almost automatically, even when your thoughts aren't on board. You absolutely have to avoid thinking about what you're doing—don't imagine any real or imagined partner, or any images of sexual practices. This is the only way you will reach a trance state where your mind only picks up stimuli coming from your cock without being distracted by other influences. These touches alone won't bring you to ejaculation—what will make you cum is remembering an earlier ejaculation.

Entirely separating pleasurable sensations from your thoughts and continuing in this way as long as you like is also possible if someone else is stroking you with their hands. But it's enough for you to just realize briefly what you're doing—and you'll cum almost on the spot!

11th Exercise

This exercise is almost like a continuation of the previous one. If you finished it by ejaculating, you might be in the mood again after an hour. You can even cum a second time. Once you have an erection it's much easier to maintain your state of arousal for longer periods of time.

The bigger "problem" in this situation can be the erection itself. In most cases, even light touches will be enough to give you an erection again. But sometimes your cock doesn't seem to answer after it's been satisfied. Completely apathetic, it just wants to rest, even though you would like to cum again.

I'll repeat what I've said before: there's no point in going through the classic motions on a cock that's already ejaculated and is now lying there fully flaccid.

In this case, an indirect stimulation, not relying on direct touch, can be much more effective. Psychological stimulation will almost always cause immediate reactions: if you're alone, porn can help.

You can ensure that psychological stimuli will carry over into physical arousal by acting as a bit of an exhibitionist, and not just as voyeur. I don't mean causing a public disturbance, since you're at home and shouldn't be standing naked on your balcony. But just the thought that someone could see you from a window across the way can be enough to set the process in motion: you're no longer just a spectator, but an actor as well—two aspects of visual stimuli that function similarly to the way sadism and masochism do on another level.

All you need to do is stroke your naked body a bit, and you will accomplish what direct efforts with your hand certainly wouldn't have.

Lie down on your bed again, and place your thumb and index finger at the base of your cock after pulling back your foreskin. Your cock will seem very naked now, and even if it's still flaccid it will be upright. Without moving your fingers, start making jerking strokes from back to front, moving your cock in rhythmic beats. While doing this, continue pulling the skin on your cock downwards. This way, you will start to get an erection—but only if your movements remain very even. When you're about halfway between your original softness and a full erection, you can start masturbating classically. Do this slowly, making sure that pressure is now directed upwards rather than downwards. This means you squeeze your cock harder when your hand moves up towards the glans. Just before you reach your cock head, stop the stroke. Don't let your foreskin touch the glans yet. Even if your erection keeps getting stronger, you can keep going for a while without feeling the desire to masturbate more forcefully. Don't rush anything—savor this pleasant state and let things get even hotter. If you continue, you could have a second orgasm soon. The following movement can help you to noticeably extend your enjoyment. It's not very simple to learn this technique. It requires finesse and flexibility that you might not have at first. But even if the exercise isn't quite successful at first, and you don't get a chance to feel the full pleasure unfold, you will still feel how strong it is and you'll be ejaculating before you know it.

Position your thumb and index finger in a ring just beneath the glans, not touching the ridge. Place your fingers on your retracted foreskin. Before you place your fingers there firmly, "spin" the foreskin around the glans by pulling it as far as you can from left to right and then holding it in place. All other stimulation is accomplished with the help of the right hand.

Before you can firmly place your fingers on your shifted foreskin, the head of your cock will be filling with blood. It will almost look as if you're choking it. From then on, these two fingers won't move. All they have to do is maintain medium pressure in their place. Open your hand, stretching out your three other fingers. With what follows, it's not so difficult to perform the stimulation as it is to maintain it.

Don't lean your elbow against anything. With your wrist and forearm, make a fast rotating motion in a very small radius, always around the cock's axis. Your stretched-out fingers, which will now beat against your cock, will make the feeling even more arousing.

This stimulation will seem similar to the previous exercise, but the fingers are positioned quite differently, and your elbow isn't propped up against anything.

The urge to cum will soon be overpowering: if you don't watch out, two or three seconds will be enough—especially if you allow your mind to be impressed by this completely novel stimulation.

In order to give yourself the opportunity to get used to this pleasure before ejaculating—and therefore withstand this phase even longer—you have to turn your mind off and completely forget what your fingers are doing. Furthermore, you need to completely relax all your muscles and bring yourself into a state of weightlessness.

You can use this truly astounding grip to cum a third time with equally strong sensations. It won't stop working until you're completely spent!

12th Exercise

Before I begin this final chapter about dry masturbation, I want to repeat something again: the most sensitive area of the penis is the ridge of the glans. More exactly: on an erect penis, the most sensitive part is the side of the ridge that the retracted foreskin touches. This is important in order to realize that, next to psychological factors and different masturbation techniques, this area determines whether someone has a tendency to ejaculate prematurely or not, whether his plateau phase lasts shorter or longer, and whether ejaculation is sped up.

If your hand—or, above all, the inner side of your thumb—strokes against the ridge of the glans, it will cause overwhelming arousal despite the protection of the foreskin, shortening your masturbation and thus the phase of true pleasure. On the contrary, if the hand stops just below the ridge of the glans, it will be easier to maintain an erection while extending pleasure and delaying ejaculation. It's not until you've reached the trance state I'm about to explain that these cautionary procedures are no longer necessary.

The exercise I'm about to suggest to you is certainly the most refined and difficult of the ones I've described—but it's also the most effective.

Lie down on your back in bed, relaxing your whole body. Keep your legs slightly spread. You can reach a state of arousal however you like: with simple methods if that's enough, or with one of the methods from the exercise in the first chapter if you're not feeling easily aroused.

As soon as you have an erection, masturbate very evenly and slowly without squeezing your cock too tight: it's important that you do this with your left hand, without touching your glans. Your strokes should be very short and always end just beneath the glans.

At the same time, make sure that your thoughts are not concentrated on what you're doing. Don't think of anything in particular. It's best if you close your eyes. Don't forget that looking at your erect cock for a second or two is more stimulating than two minutes of masturbation with your eyes closed. This is most important at the beginning, in order to keep from losing control. It's much harder to hold back your rising cum in this early stage. For this reason alone you should avoid adding visual stimuli on top of your hand strokes.

A simple trick to help keep you from thinking of anything in particular is to hold your head still while imagining that you're turning it slowly back and forth. Concentrate entirely on the imagined completion of this motion, which should calm you down and distract you from your hand's actions. If you succeed in not interrupting these thoughts, you will achieve the proper "distance" from the sensations that are about to flood through you. This distance alone makes it possible for you to withstand the sensations. As soon as you notice that you're about to shoot—just two or three seconds before—concentrate even more on your inner state. Shut your eyelids tight and hold your breath. At the same time, continue masturbating slightly lower on the shaft, closer to the base. The urge will subside quickly. If that doesn't work right away, squeeze your cock a bit. Afterwards, you can keep going as before until the next wave rises, which you can stop the same way. After the next two or three alarm signals you can take your other hand and begin alternating back and forth. Then start again only masturbating with the ring formed by your index finger and thumb. You can tense and relax your ass cheeks, your stomach and chest muscles as well, stroking more forcefully at the same time, so your cock feels like it's almost being torn off. Then relax again and masturbate more slowly, with less pressure, restricting yourself to the lower part of your cock.

The first drops of pre-cum will have appeared by now. Now you can take a break for a while if you like. Your erection won't subside. When you touch your cock after the break, you'll be astounded how easily you can maintain and dominate the sexual pressure. Your cock will seem to reach a lightly prickling rigidity. At this point you no longer need to distract your thoughts from your strokes. You will feel as though you're floating and what's happening will pass over you, even though you perceive it very clearly.

Now you will reach the point where you no longer even feel the "driven" automatism of your masturbation. In this state, your masturbating hand won't seem to belong to you anymore.

Sometimes in this state you will only sense the reality of your actions and arousal because your balls are numb. The pleasure will make you almost dizzy. If you return your thoughts back to what you're doing, at the same time intensifying your strokes, the orgasm will seem unstoppable.

By reaching a plateau phase of unrestricted length—which is only possible because you turned off your mind—you have now experienced that a long-lasting climax is unrelated to the short orgasm during ejaculation.

Extended Masturbation
with Lube

1st Exercise

In contrast to masturbating with a dry penis, which is probably beloved by all, masturbating with lube isn't every man's thing.

Some men experience discomfort from the sensations it causes, while some think it's the nicest feeling there is. Some men quickly feel uneasy doing it and just want to stop, but for others there's no difference between this kind of masturbation and any other. And still others find masturbating with lotion or oil to be preferable.

The reason for these vastly different feelings is, for the most part, purely "mechanical."

During masturbation with lube, the hand slips directly over the unprotected glans, which is no longer covered by the foreskin as usual. This direct arousal through rubbing can overly sensitize the cock head, causing an irritation that's almost painful. Others, particularly men for whom lube is something new, will feel that using it doesn't increase their pleasure or make them last longer, but rather leads them to an unusually early ejaculation. Let it be said that it takes a few exercises to get used to the feeling. Any man who finds the sensation uncomfortable should try it more than once.

For many men, it's impossible to last longer than one or two minutes when using lube; a few strokes can be enough to make them cum. The following exercises will be the best "therapy": every man can convince himself that the hand obeys when the mind really wants it to. If you continually remind yourself of this fact, you can change the method of stimulation however you like in order to let your feelings of pleasure grow very slowly. This can't be said of a cock or an ass, whose erotic power is much stronger than a masturbating hand.

On the other hand—and this is a justified comparison—a hand is a much more refined tool than an ass. For example, in the following exercises you can completely ignore the tip of your cock with your hand—avoid touching it altogether, which of course isn't possible in anal intercourse.

You can simply apply the lube directly to your penis, whether it's flaccid or hard. Almond oil is well-suited, since it only has a light smell.

Lie down again, fully relaxed, with your legs lightly spread. Now oil your cock from top to bottom—and don't leave out your balls and pubic hair. It's better to use too much than too little.

With your two lubed hands, massage very softly and evenly. Don't start an even jerking motion: the point here is to send out a feeling of universal arousal that's not concentrated in any particular place. Soon you will have a strong erection. You should also avoid any up-and-down motions. Instead, massage with your whole palm, touching your cock and balls, stroking them, cupping them.

These hand grips are very sensual. Oddly enough, you'll feel as if your cock is much bigger than it actually is. You could keep up with this for an hour and still feel a strong and completely controlled desire. That's one of the biggest advantages to masturbation with lube: it's easier to make strong soft strokes that keep the cock aroused without automatically giving in to the urge to go faster.

Don't forget what the previous exercises said about concentrating and relaxing your muscles, and remember to aim your focus inward rather than on your cock. A last security precaution: if you want to keep doing this as long as possible, your legs need to remain in their relaxed starting position. Here are some stimulations you can try out. The order is up to you, depending on whether you want to heighten your desire or suppress it a little:

Alternate sliding your hands along your cock shaft, always starting at the base and ending at the cock head, which in this case will be entirely covered by the foreskin. In other words, only make the upward motion of classic masturbation. Once every ten times or so, stroke from top to bottom. Afterwards, stroke your cock very softly without touching the glans. Your hand should move over the skin of your cock without the skin itself moving. Alternate between your right and left hand, each time massaging your balls with the other hand.

Or you can lay your left thumb on top of your cock, down at the base, and press firmly, making your penis lie horizontal. With your right hand, masturbate very slowly, strong enough this time for your hand to move your skin. At first, stop beneath the glans, later, you can work this into the motion. But make sure not to cum too quickly! Don't forget the previous advice here either: if you feel like you're about to cum, you have to have the willpower to stop stroking right away. This won't harm your erection, which will stay the way it is for a while. Once you start up again, you will be glad to notice that you can handle these various pleasures without wanting to cum right away. The "scare" seems to be over.

Now you can take up the grip from the start of this exercise again, the upwards motion from the base to the glans. The more your arousal heightens, the more you should repeat an upwards stroke that doesn't make the skin on your cock move too much. In the end, start with regular up-and-down strokes.

As soon as these movements have become very even and you have the sense that you can control your arousal with relative ease, take your balls in your hand. This should pull the skin on your cock down noticeably. With your other hand, continue masturbating the full length of your cock, including the head. Change your speed and pressure from time to time. You could also take a break now, use your other hand or subdue your horniness a bit by stimulating yourself in a way that's easier to handle. In any case, you're now in the right place to dominate your instincts: you can steer your own arousal and enjoy it fully.

2ⁿᵈ Exercise

This exercise for masturbating with lube—which is best to try while lying down—offers you some particularly refined stimulations and hand movements.

But if you haven't followed the previous exercises strictly and exactly (and achieved satisfactory results) this exercise won't immediately bring you any success.

This exercise isn't just about relaxing your muscles and distracting your thoughts, which are methods you are getting to know by now, but rather about "technical mechanisms" that are quite odd and, above all, a huge turn-on.

The beginning of this exercise is identical to the previous one. It's better to put the lube on when your cock is still flaccid. Then provoke an erection with rather firm grips, massages, and pulling on your balls. This is better than simply calling on the typical jerking-off motions for help. Make sure your posture is very relaxed: spread your legs slightly and keep your eyes shut for the entire exercise. And don't forget how important it is to keep a "mental distance" from what's happening.

Grab the middle of your cock, between root and head, with your left thumb and index finger. Both fingers should be stretched out. Grab with your right thumb and index finger from the other side, in the same position. Your fingers are now surrounding your cock like two "tongs."

From now on, carry out two contrary motions at the same time: the left "tong" makes clockwise circular motions horizontally, while the right fingers go the opposite directions. Your left hand should wander from the middle up to the ridge of the glans.

At first, these strokes should be very slow and even, with little pressure. This way you can achieve a strong erection, "irreversible" so to speak. You can keep going as long as you want—nothing is going to happen, except that you will get hornier and hornier. In this state of arousal, you won't want to jump ahead. Later, you can increase the pressure in your fingers bit by bit, but just now they're like a double wrench clamping your cock and heightening your pleasure. From time to time, change the direction of your strokes, make them slower or exert less pressure. Then go faster again, press harder.

After a while you can refine this first stimulating stroke by continuing it with your left hand at the base of your cock while your right thumb and index finger masturbate in the classic style.

More and more, increase the pressure with your right hand as your left hand continues masturbating.

This is when the third stimulation—which is not very easy to perform—comes into play.

Stroke your cock with your full left hand. Stroke with your right hand as well, but only with a ring formed by your thumb and index finger. Your left hand starts at the base of your cock and doesn't go farther than the bottom of the head. The ring starts in the middle and moves to the top of the cock.

Both strokes go in the same direction, though slightly delayed. When your left hand reaches the bottom, the ring should have just started moving downwards and vice versa. Do all this without taking breaks, very evenly. With this stroke as well, you should increase the pressure in both of your hands after a few minutes, but you can also isolate the hands if you like.

Now you will feel the urge to cum. With both hands, which are now parallel to your cock, slide in the direction of your ball sack. Be very insistent with your middle fingers, sliding them underneath your balls and then moving them back upwards to the head. Keep your thumbs on top, making the same top-to-bottom motion, which they will repeat quite a few times. The pressure should soon subside.

Now you can start pleasuring yourself again, and each time you feel close to ejaculating, simply interrupt with the same process. Of course, you can alter rhythm and pressure as you like.

At this point you can return to the first stroke, only this time it should be more energetic and a bit jerky. Then start up with the previous method again, turning it into a motion of your whole right hand, which should slide over your entire shaft including the glans while your left hand pulls the skin on your cock back by closing tightly around the balls. If you feel cum rising again, use the method I just described, and the urge will fade.

Nothing is stopping you now from continuing however you like, either taking up one of the previously described strokes or deciding to blow your load.

To finish off, here's a stroke that will totally get you off:

Close your left-hand fingers firmly around your balls and pull the skin of your cock down as far as possible. Lay the ring formed by your first two right-hand fingers at the base of your cock, bending your wrist and positioning the ring upside-down: your other fingers will automatically close around the shaft. Now masturbate by turning the ring in a half-circle from left to right with every upwards motion. Increase the pressure, particularly when you reach the ridge of the glans. When you reach the base again, make a half-circle in the other direction.

3rd Exercise

The next two exercises describe what is most likely the most elaborate form of masturbation there is.

In order to make it easier to try, I've separated the technique into two exercises. But if you can "handle" it, you can do one after the other.

These exercises are the essence of transcendent masturbation: they encompass the entire book, so to speak.

In order to combine elementary sexuality with higher technique, it's important to run through the various learning stages in the previous chapters. Very few men are capable of stroking themselves to such unbelievable effect in the state right before climax.

Just for comparison: it's not unusual to spend two hours on this kind of masturbation—and that's not even the boundary of what's possible. Which has little in common with the few minutes it normally takes to masturbate.

These two exercises contain manipulations that build strictly off of one another. If you used them in a different order, they wouldn't work. Also remember that it takes a certain amount of willpower to reach the trance state in which the plateau phase begins. Once you've conquered the first impulses to ejaculate, this willpower will gradually become less important.

For this exercise, stand upright, lubing your cock and balls once you have an erection. What's most important at first is reaching the point just before ejaculation three or four times, and conquering the urge.

Each time when you've passed this point and conquered the urge to ejaculate, it will take longer until you have to interrupt yourself again. Oddly enough, you will also have to take a longer break before you start again.

You've got to be "strong" in two ways here: first, when it's about choosing the right time to stop before ejaculating—not too early and not too late—and then knowing when to continue masturbating—only when your cock has really calmed down and not before.

For this reason, you have to avoid rushing in any way that could cause you to lose control. Focus on maintaining the same mental distance and analyzing all your sensations precisely.

When you're masturbating, just use the classic strokes. Keep the rhythm quite slow, squeezing quite tightly (despite the lube) in order to pull your foreskin along at every stroke.

Remember that you've got various methods to assist you if your willpower isn't enough on its own: relaxing your muscles, squeezing the head of your cock, giving strong pressure in the ball region, and—the most effective method in a standing position—changing your leg position and resting on one leg.

4th Exercise

Now it's time to heighten your pleasure with different stimulations. The following movements will satisfy you intensely over a long period of time without causing you the fear of shooting uncontrollably.

The order of these movements and their exact use will take you into a plateau phase of unlimited length.

Lube yourself up well again, massaging your cock and balls solely with your right hand in upwards movements. Don't be afraid of giving lots of strong pulls. Then do the same thing with your left hand. This first phase should last a long time. Even if your erection stays constantly hard, there's no chance of ejaculation.

Now you can gradually add in some downward strokes that pull the foreskin down from the head of your cock.

The following stimulation is better with your left hand:

With your index finger and the middle of your thumb placed naturally left and right of your cock, give the entire length of your cock shaft (excluding the head) circular massaging strokes. Make sure you massage very slowly, pressing much more firmly when stroking down than when stroking up. If you do this massage correctly, you shouldn't have to fear an unexpected ejaculation.

Continue this massage for a long time, until you feel a kind of numbness at the base of your cock.

Now make the same circular motion with the same fingers, but this time counter-clockwise. Press harder when you stroke up on the right side of the shaft and weaker when you slide down the left.

After a while you can alternate between the two contrary motions. Then go back to the first kind of massage for almost as long.

Now lube yourself up and again repeat the strokes, alternating between your hands and stroking three times from bottom to top before you stroke once from top to bottom and reveal the glans.

Bit by bit this stimulation will grow more intense, until it's almost "brutal" by the end. Your state of arousal will now be constant. If you feel the urge to ejaculate, simply go slower or don't press as hard.

You can now simply masturbate in the classic way by sliding your whole hand over your lubed, fully erect cock. You will see that you'll be extremely horny without wanting to ejaculate at all. The glans, which is already extremely sensitized, can now handle an extra touch: the stroke from the last exercise where the upside-down right hand carries out a slightly delayed up-and-down motion.

This stroke will bring you closer to the point where ejaculation seems almost unavoidable. You won't be able to continue like this for very long. You can keep your desire in check a bit by repeating the hand grips described here. You can even do this several times, since the order in which they're described will sustain your arousal without letting your desire for orgasm grow too great.

This can be continued until you reach the point where it's very difficult to break off each stimulation and to delay orgasm without frustration.

It's not an exaggeration to say that you will truly only cum when you want to.

If you want to increase these sensations (especially just before you reach the end of the game) you can add another one or two rings around your cock.

Or you can rub oil over yourself again, this time even on your upper thighs, stomach, and chest muscles. And if you decide you want to cum, your lubed-up nipples will increase your pleasure immensely.

Need I mention that your orgasm will be particularly overpowering and that it will take longer than usual before you can start again?

Controlled Ejaculation

After the exercises in this third section, you will be well-equipped to obtain full control of your ejaculations. In order to do this, however, you've first got to master the techniques for prolonging masturbation that were explained in the last chapters.

The following exercises are ordered in a particular way, progressively building up to stronger, more intense stimulations. This progression can serve as a good test of your resistance in a heightened state of arousal. What's most important is that these exercises don't focus on the stroke you use to arouse your penis, but rather on which area of your cock you stimulate.

It's always easier to resist stimulation at the base of the cock. Stimulating the shaft is also quite bearable. It becomes more difficult when stimulating the head or the entire cock.

In the following exercises, not only are these various regions examined, but so are your reactions and the quality of your perceptions. The level of intensity in your pleasure will depend on whether you're completely relaxed or not, and whether you're completely concentrating on the stimulation, even perhaps strengthening your concentration visually with the help of a mirror. Such pleasure-heightening methods naturally make it more difficult to withstand the exercise for a longer period of time.

Of course, the intensity of your visual arousal is completely dependent on what you're looking at while you're jerking off. If you look at your glans from above, this will clearly heighten your arousal; looking at the underside and frenulum can help you last longer without losing control.

It's similar when it comes to which hand you use: assuming you use it from the start, it's easier for right-handed men to reach a state of arousal with their left hand, even though it's normally the more awkward hand. Certain strokes with this hand can even cause a particularly intense feeling.

1st Exercise

This is definitely the simplest exercise. Although you will reach a maximum arousal with a minimum of touching, this is even suited for men who tend to shoot very quickly.

Lay on your back. Don't lube up your penis yet. Of course, make sure to be as relaxed as possible. When you're masturbating, focus only on the lower half of your cock, from the base to the middle. This means that from the very start, you only stimulate this part.

In the first chapter, where erectile difficulties were discussed, you will find several stimulations that deal with this region. If you don't like any of them, simply choose the one you assume will work best. But make sure to avoid coming too close to the cock head—or to avoid touching it—as much as you can.

This is probably the most effective method: masturbate with your index finger and thumb in a ring after pulling your foreskin back from the glans, only stroking a small part of the shaft. At first, the movement should be very slow and soft, then it should grow faster and firmer. Your strokes should never go higher than the middle of your cock. If you've been looking at your cock until now, close your eyes as soon as you feel your erection beginning.

Concentrate all your thoughts on the sensations that arise as your cock becomes erect.

Continue jerking without taking a break. You can also change hands. With your other hand, you can massage your balls or stimulate another part of your body, perhaps your nipples or whatever feels best.

Once you're fully erect, close your whole hand around your cock. Your strokes should stay small. Don't forget: this stimulation is only aimed at the lower half of your shaft. However, even with this seemingly restricted movement, there are opportunities for variation: you can grip harder when you stroke up or when your hand is moving down. You can go faster or slower, grip more firmly or open your hand more. It will feel as though you wouldn't be able to ejaculate now even if you wanted to. As turned on as you already are, you will want stronger stimulations. Don't give in to this desire—resist the urge until you're done jerking off. After a little while it will no longer be difficult to stay strong. If you keep going this way until your cock is full of blood, you will want to continue with the same strokes. Now is the time to add the "voyeuristic element" by adding a mirror to the mix. If you've followed all the instructions until now, this extra source of arousal won't change your state too much. You've already overcome the critical phase, virtually without noticing it.

At first, place yourself directly across from the mirror. Be sure not to cheat: don't look at your cock directly, only look at it through the mirror.

The "view" of your body lying down and your erect cock (which looks larger at the top, since you're only working part of the shaft) will make you even hornier. You will notice that even though you feel hornier, you still have things fully under control.

Now the first drops of pre-cum will appear.

If the idea pops into your head that you want to shoot, there's an easy way to counteract this: simply close your eyes while you keep jerking off.

Also, no matter how aroused you are, you can "shut off" your mind, as explained in the last chapter.

Once you've reached this dangerous point, don't resort to the normal strokes under any circumstances—two or three normal masturbation strokes and you would lose control entirely. In this case it would be wrong to claim that you really wanted to cum. Now bring an extra difficulty into play: place yourself parallel to the mirror. In this position, you can hardly cheat—unless you do it intentionally. The exercise now becomes more difficult, since it's more arousing in a way to see yourself from the side. This new position is a kind of bridge between the previous one and the one that follows.

Now you can see your cock from the side, protruding from your hand. Remember here what was said before: seeing the ridge of the glans causes a more intense sensation. For this reason, fixate mostly on the head of your cock, not on the rest or even your hand.

You can use any of the previous variations and grips, only this time your arousal won't overwhelm you as quickly as it did before. It will increase on its own. You won't have the urge to heighten it with different grips. You will feel so proud of what you've managed so far that you won't even have the urge to cum anymore. Those who are still not quite "under control," despite all the cautionary procedures and stages, can simply think of those additional methods that will make it possible to delay orgasm even more: closing the eyes and completely relaxing the muscles.

After your arousal hasn't increased for a while, you can abandon the mirror and look at yourself directly as you masturbate. It will be particularly arousing how hard your cock is, and how thick the head of your cock has become.

Without these preparations, you would not have been able to reach this last stage. The power you have over your masturbation will make you hornier and hornier.

In the last few minutes, you were masturbating almost automatically. Now you can turn your willpower back on.

The easiest thing now is to keep stroking with your hand. You can do this right away or gradually. But you will get the best results if you just keep going the way you were before, adding your mind to the mix and letting fantasies, images, and previous orgasms come into play. Tell yourself that you would like to cum now.

You can support this mental determination by playing with your muscles and pressing your upper thighs together. Now it's full speed ahead, come what may!

Your ejaculation won't disobey you anymore—you will be the one who decides.

2nd Exercise

This exercise will make it possible for you to go a step further, and you will see how much more of a turn-on it is. It will still be possible to keep your masturbation fully in control and to decide when you ejaculate—so long you follow these steps.

In practice, this exercise is very different from the last one, since three stages of pleasure follow, one after the other, without it being necessary to return to a stage once you've passed it. Here there are two or three repetitions. This is the only way you will be able to sustain your arousal for a nearly unlimited time.

The position of your body is the same as in the previous exercise.

After you've stimulated yourself lightly to begin with, you can masturbate quite normally, making sure to shut your eyes. Try out a bunch of variations, mixing short and long strokes—but not too long. When you masturbate quickly, extend your strokes far, touching the whole cock. When you go slowly, restrict your strokes to one part of the shaft.

Switching hands can have very pleasant effects. But in this phase, you should build up your arousal with just one hand.

Once you feel that your horniness has increased, don't make any more fast strokes. Instead, restrict yourself to slow ones in such a small range that you can hardly feel them anymore. Release the pressure almost completely.

This alone should subdue your arousal a bit, particularly if you relax your ass muscles at the same time.

As you go on, concentrate your jerking solely on the upper half of the cock. Without changing your speed at first, increase the pressure significantly. Now restrict your up-and-down strokes even more, only touching the head, letting the foreskin slide back and forth over it. Start going faster and grip more tightly.

If you reach the phase just before ejaculation again, stop everything and place your hand at the base of your cock right away, masturbating slowly and lightly there for a few minutes. At the same time, distract your thoughts.

Up until now, your eyes were closed. But now you should look at your hand in the mirror. It's holding your cock. Make sure to keep your muscles completely relaxed. Now you can masturbate with strokes that grow firmer, faster, and extend further, using more pressure when you get to the head, nearly squeezing it with your thumb and index finger. But don't wait until your arousal has grown so great that you can't control it! If you feel it's getting dangerous, close your thumb and index finger firmly in a ring for a few seconds without moving. Breathe deeply in and out as slow as you can, concentrating your thoughts fully on controlling your breath. Now close your eyes again.

These distraction maneuvers will make your arousal subside a bit.

Now repeat all the stages of this exercise from the start, maintaining the order strictly. This time you should be able to withstand each of the three phases for a much longer time without feeling the need to ejaculate right away. By concentrating on controlling all of your sensations, you should be able to avoid taking any breaks, even very short ones.

Once you're in the third phase, you can "cheat" for a minute. Look directly at your cock head. It will immediately become clear to you how much more of a turn-on this sight is than the image in the mirror. Fixate on the mirror again, following your hand's extended up-and-down strokes until you feel a clear spike in arousal.

Now close your eyes again and start from the beginning, this time without paying too much attention to your breathing. If you decide that you don't want to cum at the end of this repetition, you will reach the trance state where your sensations are freed from any "emotional imagination" in your brain. You will simply feel like savoring this state longer rather than coming.

You can extend the first phase even longer by imagining what you are doing with your eyes still closed. If you concentrate enough on this visual image, you will feel even more pleasure. Once you reach the stage of stroking your cock head, you will experience a kind of permanent orgasm—which wouldn't have been possible the first time around.

But even now you will remain concentrated enough to reach the last phase, in which you look at yourself in the mirror and get confirmation of what you were just imagining.

Don't blow your load until now, until you've really reached the limits of what you can handle.

3rd Exercise

Now we're reaching the highest level of resistance against prematature ejaculation—under particularly difficult circumstances, no less: lying down, with a dry penis.

All three phases are enriched with visual stimulation, which makes your horniness even harder to handle.

If you try this exercise twice in the same day, it will naturally last longer the second time. Your position in front of the mirror should be independent of how horny you are to start with—and how strong your "resistance power" is.

When your cock is "at attention," and you've mastered the last exercises without a problem, lie down in lengthwise in front of the mirror. If this isn't possible, sit across from it; in this position, your own image will help you handle your own horniness better. The more you can handle this stimulation, the longer you will be able to last if someone else is masturbating you.

As soon as you have an erection, start stimulating your glans for a while. This stage will be more difficult if you achieve an erection through traditional masturbation. Make sure not to use the classic strokes for too long!

Start masturbating with the familiar ring formed by your

thumb and index finger. The movement should be slow and quite firm.

With the help of this tight ring, strangle your cock and stretch it out. As soon as the head is more aroused, you can let your fore-skin partly or fully slide over it with every upwards stroke.

Make sure your visual stimulation only comes from looking in the mirror, as it's the only way to make the stimulation last longer. Don't take your eyes off the mirror until you've managed to avoid ejaculation at last three times, even though you will be even more intensely aroused each time.

Now you can look directly at yourself, continuing the above strokes for a few minutes. Gradually replace the ring with your whole hand. Make your strokes faster and longer.

In order to keep your arousal under control even longer, make the following changes: At first, your up-and-down strokes will touch your whole cock, slowly, evenly and with not too much pressure. Gradually, switch to a shorter stroke, faster and firmer and above all restricted to the base of the cock so that your hand is beating against your balls. Now alternate this stroke with a slower version of the first, grasping more firmly with each upwards movement than with the reverse.

After you've kept going normally, with slow and even strokes, reverse the whole thing: on the way down, masturbate with short, slow and firm strokes—on the way up with fast strokes that are less firm. Although you will maintain your state of arousal, you won't feel the urge to ejaculate as quickly as the last times. You will even feel the opposite effect: the clearer the difference between the normal up-and-down strokes and these varyingly strong strokes, the more diffused the urge will be.

You can maintain this second phase for a while. The whole time, watch your hand and the part of the cock it's stroking. This will enable you to control your horniness.

Now is the last phase of the exercise, where you will decide to ejaculate.

While you keep jerking normally, start looking at your glans every now and then. At first, only give it fleeting glances, then fixate on your shaft for a while. At the same time, stimulate the head area with your hand. To make it clearer: When your hand is approaching the head, you should fixate on the shaft. Once your hand moves away, you can look at the head.

You can gradually let your eyes rest on the glans more and more, shortening the amount of time your hand stimulates it.

Over time, you will start to get used to the sight, although it's the most sensitive spot, the one that's most receptive to touch.

If you want to delay and strengthen ejaculation even more, start masturbating the head alone, fixating your eyes on the now-visible lower half of your cock.

When you want to cum, increase speed and pressure and focus your gaze on the head of your cock.

4ᵗʰ Exercise

The standing exercises don't look much different from the others. What sets them apart is that it's much easier to lose control of your ejaculation while standing. But if you take into mind the following tips and stimulate yourself according to the instructions, you will be able to control yourself fully. This will only be possible if you bring your whole willpower into play just before the point of no return.

With this exercise, we're going deeper into "transcendent masturbation." Your ejaculation will bend entirely to your will.

After you've gotten your cock hard, don't keep masturbating in the usual way. This familiar gesture won't really allow you to make it through all of the phases. So don't depend on that "secure feeling."

Stand up with your legs relaxed (make sure to keep thinking about relaxing all your muscles), close your eyes and stroke just the tip of your cock. But don't use any of the variations from the first exercise in this chapter.

Simply let the tip of your cock slide through the ring formed by your thumb and index finger. Spread your other fingers. If you like, you can vary this simple movement by gripping harder at first, then stroking faster with less pressure.

Once your erection is really hard, you can get ready for actual masturbation.

With very short thrusts, pull the ring downward. Repeat this movement several times, keeping the rhythm very strict the whole time. Each time you reach the cock's base, place the ring back up on the glans without touching your cock during the upwards motion.

In other words, you're only doing half of the usual jerking stroke. If you want to keep your rising arousal in check, reverse the direction and stroke upwards—but only on the bottom half of your cock. This upwards movement needs to be quite a bit slower. At the same time, make sure to pull the ring together tightly, nearly squeezing your cock.

You can alternate these two movements: the first makes you hornier, the other will bring you back down.

As long as your eyes are closed, you won't ejaculate, despite an insane level of arousal. Wait until you're very secure and your strokes have gotten markedly faster; then you can open your eyes and look at yourself in the mirror.

Look first from the front, then in profile—and all the while keep stroking. If you change positions, you will notice that it's more arousing to look at yourself from the side. If you feel like you're about to cum, but would like to continue, simply start up again with the stroke described above, but this time very slow and even, without pressure. You'll see that the pressure subsides, and you can keep going.

The danger won't be securely behind you until you've reached and overcome the point just before ejaculation at least three times.

Then it's entirely up to you whether you want to or not, and you will sense that it's become much easier to maintain control. Once you really feel secure, you can look at yourself directly, not just in the mirror. After just a few seconds, you'll feel your arousal spike.

Once you've reached this point, you can alternate the ring strokes and masturbating with your whole hand. As long as you restrict yourself to the lower half of your cock, you will be able to hold back ejaculation without trouble. It's your decision what you want to do next ...

5th Exercise

This is the final exercise for dry masturbation and full control of ejaculation. It's also the most difficult. If you succeed in controlling your arousal for a long period of time, you've really made progress.

As soon as you have an erection, start masturbating the head of your cock with short strokes, at first standing in front of the mirror with your legs lightly spread to allow your muscles to relax. Don't use too much pressure with the ring formed by your thumb and index finger—instead, make your strokes faster.

In order to avoid being overpowered by real arousal, stand so you can see yourself and the whole length of your cock in profile. This means, if the mirror is to your left, masturbate with your right hand.

Now make the up-and-down strokes of the ring jerkier, with more pressure. Right away, the urge to shoot will arise. Interrupt everything by following the tips from the last exercises. Since you're standing with your legs spread, it will be enough to rest your weight on one leg, which should be your left. Tense all the muscles in your left leg while keeping your right leg fully relaxed. On the spot, this will put the brakes on your rising semen. Now let go of your cock for two or three seconds.

Start up again, this time with your left hand. Fix your eyes on the head of your cock. When you feel ejaculation approaching again, do the same thing as before. Only this time, put your weight on your right leg.

As you continue, masturbate slower and with less pressure. Soon you'll want to cum again, and you can overcome the urge the same way—except you won't interrupt your stroking this time, and you should keep looking at the head of your cock. Let your thoughts wander for a few moments until you've calmed down. Now you can really masturbate while watching your hand and cock at the same time. If you've followed all the instructions, you will reach a calm phase where it's practically impossible to feel an immediate urge to ejaculate, even though your erection is very firm and you are constantly masturbating.

You can bring your masturbation to an end by simply using the same hand motions from the beginning of this exercise—with the big difference that you're now looking at the head of your cock. If your strokes were touching the entire shaft before, they should now be restricted to a small radius on the lower part; then use more pressure as your hand moves upwards.

As soon as you bend forward, stick your ass out and push your cock as close to horizontal as you can. Your pleasure will multiply. You will almost reach the edge of what you can handle. If you want to subdue your arousal a bit, just change your pressure slightly, stand up a bit straighter again, and the tension will be much more bearable.

Then you can keep going as before. This time, use less pressure at first and then increase, interrupting your even up-and-down strokes with a downward stroke over your entire shaft.

The position of your wrist will have to change slightly, no longer extending straight out from your arm. Soon you will feel a clear increase of arousal. If you want to cum now, all you need to do is concentrate your strokes to a half-inch area around the head of your cock, then bend slightly forward and push your cock down horizontally.

6th Exercise

You will quickly determine that the following two exercises are quite similar to the previous ones. The big difference is that these exercises use lube. This alone makes some extra explanations necessary.

It's up to you whether you want to apply the oil when you're still soft, or if you want to wait until you've got a hard-on. But if you want to focus on stimulating the head of your cock at first, you shouldn't put the lube on until you have an erection. As before, the first part of this exercise is the simplest. You'll see that you can last even longer with this one.

Lie down on your back, fully relaxed, with your face towards the mirror. Only masturbate the base of your cock, again with your thumb and index finger in a ring. In this spot, and with a layer of lube, this touch will seem pretty weak at first. Feel free to use your right hand. When you stroke, the ring should move, but not your skin. On the up stroke, make short downward thrusts with your wrist. Don't pass the middle of your cock. These thrusts, as well as the entire act of masturbation, should be quite slow and even. While your cock grows harder, pull the ring tighter—even very tight at times. Lay your left thumb down in the small indentation between your cock and pubic hair, pushing as hard as you can.

This will have two effects: the pressure will increase, and the skin on your cock will be pulled downwards and thus unable to follow the motion of your fingers as they slip along it. Open your eyes and look at your cock in the mirror: you will be more aroused, but still fully under control.

Add another finger to the ring, then another. In the end, your whole hand will be closed around your cock. Depending on how large your cock is, your radius of action will be more or less restricted. But even if you can only make very short strokes, don't let them get close to the head of your cock.

Now you will almost want to cum again. You can cut off this urge very easily, since it will arise gradually. Simply stop stroking, squeeze your cock tight, and close your eyes or think about something else.

When you start up again, work in the following change: Lay your three middle fingers on top of your cock with your thumb and pinky on the bottom side. Your left thumb should stay in its position, supported by the left index finger, which should press on the underside of the base of the cock.

Now you can watch yourself and increase your speed, although the pressure of the masturbating hand should stay quite light. Even though you're very aroused, you will be able to handle this state for a long time. Then you will feel you're about to cum again. If you don't want to ejaculate yet, press the fingers of your left hand firmly together without interrupting the strokes of your right hand. Your arousal will subside.

Now keep stimulating yourself with your thumb and index finger in a ring, and then with your whole hand. You can change hands, varying speed and pressure—and you won't cum until you want to.

7th Exercise

The knowledge imparted in this exercise is particularly useful if you want to cum again after having sex, even though only an hour or two have passed.

If your first ejaculation was very satisfying, your cock will now be "satisfied" and fairly "exhausted." For the most part, classic back-and-forth strokes won't offer any results. But there are so many things to do with your hand that you should be able to bring your cock to attention.

As I've already explained several times, a vibrating motion works much faster in this state than the usual up-and-down. And if you use lotion or oil while doing that, success is guaranteed.

First pull your foreskin back and grab your cock with all five fingers as if you were holding a pencil. Pull your skin as far down as possible and start making very fast vibrations through short, quick twists of your wrist. Your wrist should be bent; otherwise you won't be able to make any real vibrations.

The faster these vibrations are, and the longer they last, the quicker you will feel a change. Usually, even ten seconds is enough for the beginnings of an erection.

Now is the time to lube up your cock completely. Then keep going with the vibrations. This time place your right thumb and index finger way down at the base of your cock, increasing the stimulation by pressing down regularly.

Once your erection is fully standing, start the usual back-and-forth strokes over the whole length of the shaft. Hold your skin back by keeping your left hand at the base of your cock. As long as the head of your cock isn't fully aroused and full of blood, you shouldn't touch it. Otherwise you can use any of the variations you've now learned: you can press your upper thighs together, tense your ass, then relax all your muscles again, increase or lower pressure and speed—whichever you like. Your arousal will remain constant, even if you raise or lower the intensity by trying different variations. At the same time, your erection will be steady, even though you won't feel any urge to cum yet.

Only at this point should you work the head of your cock into your strokes. Alternate short precise up-and-down motions restricted to the glans with extended motions encompassing the entire shaft. With both of these, change the level of pressure as you see fit. If you've been keeping your eyes closed, you can open them now. Even while watching yourself, it should now be possible for you to extend this stage for a long time. You will only cum when you choose to.

8th Exercise

This last exercise for lying down will allow you to experience an extended erection and to masturbate longer than you ever thought possible.

If you follow the stimulations in order, you will maintain perfect control over your ejaculation and constantly-growing arousal without having to interrupt your masturbation even once. If you've properly experimented with the previous exercises, you will now be able to reach full control of your desire.

Two conditions need to be kept: First, you have to masturbate with the same hand from the start—that is, your left hand (for righties). This applies even if a partner is masturbating you. And second, you have to continue stimulating yourself—from the beginning until you start to pre-cum—without irregularities, without breaks and without any changes in your routine.

Once you've fully lubed your cock and balls (it doesn't matter whether it's soft or hard), start with the classical jerking-off strokes, fairly fast and light. Only your thumb, index, and middle finger should touch your cock.

At first, only stimulate the middle of your cock, then after a while move to the head. Your foreskin will be pulled along with this movement, but it should usually only cover the ridge of the glans. At the moment, your right hand should still be inactive. Once you have an erection, your skin will automatically become tighter. Now use less pressure with your hand so your skin doesn't move along with it any more.

As with the exercises for dry masturbation, you can gradually build up additional visual arousal: first looking through the mirror, then only looking at the bottom part of the shaft, and only afterwards concentrating on the head of your cock. You will notice that when your cock is lubed up, it's easier to control your arousal while looking in the mirror.

The first time you feel you're about to cum, simply bring your willpower into play and slow down your stroking a bit. Once the danger has passed, you can increase the pressure again without going faster—until you notice a second time that you're about to cum.

Now you can make use of the following trick: right away, turn your hand so that your thumb and index finger are lying lengthwise on your cock. Your strokes can be quite firm—the urge to ejaculate will pass quickly. As soon as you place your hand the way it was before, your arousal will heighten again and you can keep going, trying out whichever variations you like.

The following three techniques are perfect for trying one after the other. But if you're very horny, you should work little pauses in between the individual techniques.

Lube up your cock again, masturbating with your thumb and index finger formed into a ring, restricted to the base of your cock. Until you've overcome the third alarm signal, you should masturbate with your left hand. Afterwards you will also be able to control yourself if you use your right hand. As soon as your erection is half there, add another finger to the ring, and another, until you're using your whole hand. Make firm upward strokes that only reach from the base of your cock to the middle. The lube will make masturbating in only one direction easier. Each time you reach the middle of your cock, squeeze tighter and pull upwards.

At the first alarm of an approaching ejaculation, continue jerking off, restricting the ring entirely to the base of your cock and using lots of pressure. Then keep going normally. Do the same thing the second time, but don't use as much pressure. The third time, you can replace the narrow ring with your hand and make a rising motion from the base of your cock to the middle. This massage, which was first only an upwards motion, gradually changes into the classic up-and-down without you changing the pressure. You can even let the pressure gradually grow weaker until your erection subsides slightly without your cock getting smaller. Now you can change hands and continue nearly endlessly.

9th Exercise

The previous exercise focused on the base of the cock. The top part of the cock wasn't stimulated at all. One or two strokes over the head and you would have ejaculated.

But before we focus on the head, let's concentrate on the entire length of the shaft—excluding the glans. Even when the glans is full of blood, it needs time to get used to withstanding prolonged stimulation at its most sensitive spots.

It will be easier to get used to your growing arousal with your penis lubed up. By using lube, you can use more pressure over a much longer period of time, increasing your pleasure.

Masturbate with your right hand using the technique from the last exercise. This pressure "against the grain" will let your arousal grow without giving you the urge to cum right away.

This time, don't restrict your movement to the lower half of the cock; instead, your strokes should end just beneath the glans, right where the foreskin touches it.

Alternate firm, even up-and-down strokes with lighter strokes, changing speed and radius of motion as you wish. Here as well, you will need to overcome the critical phase three times. Only afterwards can you be sure of reaching a nearly boundless plateau phase.

If your movements are always even, and you don't throw in other movements in between, it will probably be unnecessary to make any abrupt pauses. Your thoughts will be able to analyze and dominate your sensations so clearly and fully that you can try out as many variations as you like without being in danger of shooting early.

Now you can alter the pressure of your strokes, first more firm in the upwards movement and weaker in the downwards movement, and then vice versa.

Thanks to the lube, you will be able to maintain this stage of arousal for much longer. After a while, you can bring the head of your cock into the stimulation, first half covered by your foreskin, then fully exposed.

10th Exercise

The third and last part of this last exercise is the climax of what you can reach with this type of self-gratification.

With your experience from the previous chapters and your practice overcoming progressively difficult phases, even men who normally ejaculate too soon should have overcome their problems.

Just so you get an idea: you can continue this type of masturbation for an hour or more—something hardly any man who pleasures himself in the typical way can claim. This is a marked increase in comparison to the first exercises in this book—particularly if you consider that this stimulation encompasses the entire penis, leaving nothing out.

As in the last two exercises, start by masturbating "against the grain," only making upward strokes. Bit by bit, add some downward strokes, so that you gradually arrive at the classic up-and-down. This time, stimulate the head of your cock from the start. It will fill more and more with blood, but you still won't feel an ejaculation approaching.

Now continue as follows:

In order to keep your posture stable, place your left forearm firmly on your hip. Then stroke your left hand along the glans and its immediate area as long as possible. This motion should use very weak pressure, and stay very even. Keep the pressure low for at least five minutes before gradually increasing it, then squeeze really firmly.

Since your glans is lubed up, it won't be covered by the foreskin anymore. Your arousal will increase without leading to ejaculation right away. If you lift your forearm from your hips, you will feel as if you're about to cum due to this altered, slightly irregular movement.

Nothing is easier than dealing with this sensation: simply press firmly at the base of your cock and then return to masturbating normally after ten or fifteen seconds, encompassing your entire cock without propping yourself up with your forearm.

After a while (you decide how long you want to keep going), go back to stimulating the glans.

Now you will reach the stage where you can masturbate classically, by using more pressure when your hand slides towards your torso. You don't need to exclude the head, but keep your foreskin fully retracted. You will reach a perfect equilibrium between arousal and the desire to cum.

Your erection is sturdy and your control is complete. Now anything is possible: you can change hands, alter speed or pressure—nothing will cause you to ejaculate unless you want to.

In this phase it's quite simple to imagine the comparison between this even back-and-forth motion and penetration …

Now it might even seem difficult for you to blow your load. But if you want to cum, all you need to do is massage your balls lightly and concentrate on the area just below your balls. Or fixate entirely on what you're doing, watch yourself and simply will it to happen! And you'll be sure to shoot in a way you've never before experienced while pleasuring yourself.